EDUCATIONAL THERAPY
IN THE
ELEMENTARY SCHOOL

(Third Printing)

EDUCATIONAL THERAPY
IN THE
ELEMENTARY SCHOOL

An Educational Approach to the
Learning Problems of Children

By

PATRICK ASHLOCK, Ed.D.
Director of Reading Instruction, Ridgewood High School
Norridge, Illinois
Lecturer in Education, Bradley University
Peoria, Illinois

and

ALBERTA STEPHEN, M.A.
Special Education Teacher, Galveston Independent School District
Department of Pediatrics, University of Texas Medical Branch
John Sealy Hospital
Galveston, Texas

With an Introduction by

N. C. Kephart, Ph.D.
Achievement Center for Children
Department of Education, Purdue University
Lafayette, Indiana

Illustrations by

Donald B. Hunter

CHARLES C THOMAS • **PUBLISHER**
Springfield • *Illinois* • *U.S.A.*

Published and Distributed Throughout the World by

CHARLES C THOMAS • PUBLISHER

Bannerstone House

301-327 East Lawrence Avenue, Springfield, Illinois, U.S.A.

Natchez Plantation House

735 North Atlantic Boulevard, Fort Lauderdale, Florida, U.S.A.

© *1966, by* CHARLES C THOMAS • PUBLISHER

Library of Congress Catalog Card Number: 66-16780

First Printing, 1966
Second Printing, 1967
Third Printing, 1970

*With THOMAS BOOKS careful attention is given to all details of manu-
facturing and design. It is the Publisher's desire to present books that are
satisfactory as to their physical qualities and artistic possibilities and
appropriate for their particular use. THOMAS BOOKS will be true to those
laws of quality that assure a good name and good will.*

Printed in the United States of America
R-1

*This book is dedicated
to the children who have taught us.*

INTRODUCTION

O UR MODERN civilization is characterized by rapid and extensive technological development. The resulting increase in complexity of modern living has in turn increased our concern for education and the preparation of our children and youth for their place in such a complex civilization. The task of the public schools has greatly increased both in quantity and quality. We must teach more complex materials and we must teach more per unit of time.

As a result, both school administrations and the general public are becoming increasingly aware of the problems of children who do not learn efficiently through the normal presentations of the classroom. No longer can we tolerate minor degrees of learning disability which, in a former generation, would have gone unnoticed. Society cannot gainfully absorb the inadequately educated individual as it formerly did and, with each succeeding year, the opportunities for utilizing his limited contributions decrease. It is time to take a close look at the problems of the child with learning disabilities and the responsibilities of the school for his welfare.

It is estimated that between 15 and 20 per cent of the children in our school population have learning problems sufficiently severe to interfere noticeably with their education. Such children, either because of inadequacies in their organisms or in their environment or in the interaction between the two, cannot learn efficiently from the normal classroom presentation of learning experiences. This is not to say that they cannot learn. In academic activities, however, they will need special attention and special help. Sometimes this special consideration will concentrate on the external aspects of the overall learning situation, modifying the home or community environment as required to improve the overall climate for learning. Sometimes the special consideration will need to be directed toward the child himself, improving basic skills and abilities to permit more rapid or more accurate

vii

learning. Sometimes the special consideration will need to be directed toward the learning experiences, altering methods of teaching or devising new ones so as to present materials in such a fashion that this child can absorb them and learn from them.

The recent extensive development of programs in special education represents an important approach to the problem. Specially devised programs have been made available to children who deviate from the average in certain identifiable ways. These special programs have altered the curriculum, the school environment and, to a lesser degree, the learner himself in an effort to develop each child's learning to the maximum of his capacity. The rapid, and in many cases almost frantic, growth of special education programs throughout the country attests the concern of both the profession and the public for maximum educational opportunities for children whose learning processes or learning rates are different.

In the main, the special education approach involves segregating children by area of exceptionality into special rooms or special schools, thereby removing them from the normal environment of the classroom and from extensive contact with their peers. For the more extremely disabled child such an approach is obviously desirable. This extremely disabled group, however, probably represents not over 3 to 5 per cent of the total number of children with learning problems which interfere with their education. It is obvious, therefore, that the great majority of disabled children will not be in need of such drastic measures. Furthermore, for them, with their lesser degrees of difficulty, the disadvantages of such segregated treatment far outweigh the advantages. The customary special education facility needs to be augmented, therefore, with the addition of other provisions not so far removed from the regular school routine which can provide the help necessary for achievement in this large group of children.

Some of the problems in the group not recommended for special education facilities will be of sufficient severity or sufficient breadth to require rather intensive specialized professional assistance such as that normally found in child clinical facilities. A clinical program is therefore required which will deal with problems of diagnosis and intensive programs of therapy over relatively short periods of time. Such clinical facilities might be provided within the school system or facilities available in other community agencies might be used. For purposes of education, however, these clinics should be more strongly oriented toward learning problems and the amelioration of learning difficulties than is common in current clinical practice.

Another large group of disabled children will display problems which are almost exclusively in the area of learning. Psychological and sociological problems will be at a minium but the difficulty seems centered in the learning situation per se and particularly in the academic learning situation. These children will not require the intensity of treatment usually associated with the child clinic but will require specialized assistance with their learning problems within the framework of the normal school program. For this group, opportunity should be provided for clinical teaching, remedial instruction or tutorial help. These services, however, need to be expanded both in quantity and quality. In quantity, provision should be made for the availability of such assistance to a much larger group of children than is the current practice. Children should be considered whose problems are not yet so great as to involve failure in grade or major behavior disturbances. Aid should be offered *before* a major breakdown occurs. In quality, more consideration should be given to the learner and his peculiar needs. In practice, such services customarily concentrate on intensification of methods of instruction. Little attention is given to deficiencies in basic skills or atypical methods of gathering or dealing with information which may characterize this child. The customary remedial program should be augmented with a great deal more attention to deficiencies in the child's learning process and to techniques and methods for remediating these deficiencies.

Even when ideal therapeutic facilities are available, the fact remains that a major proportion of disabled children will and should be dealt with in the regular classroom by the regular classroom teacher. Teacher training institutions need to incorporate into their programs of training much more information about and experience with the problems of children whose learning processes are different. Not only will the classroom teacher be required to provide all necessary aid for a large number of children with learning problems but, where aid is offered outside the classroom, the responsibility for following up and making effective the special assistance which has been provided the child rests with the classroom teacher. It is just at this point that many excellent clinical programs meet with failure. For this purpose, the classroom teacher requires much more specialized training than she receives in the customary teacher training program.

Children's learning, at least in so far as it involves academic skills, attitudes and knowledges, centers within the school. It follows that, although many other problems may contribute to the learning problem and although many other disciplines may be involved in the solution of the problem, the learning problem itself and the applied aspects of treatment are the concern of the school. The present volume makes an important contribution by outlining the total problem, within the framework of the public school, and providing guidelines for the development of augmented facilities for dealing with the entire range of learning problems in school children. As a handbook, it sketches the basic procedures through which implementation can be begun.

N. C. KEPHART, PH.D.
Achievement Center for Children
Department of Education
Purdue University
Lafayette, Indiana

PREFACE

Educational Therapy in the Elementary School is an attempt to draw together the relevant findings of other disciplines which deal, in whole or in part, with the learning problems of children. Special education, psychology, remedial teaching, medicine, and other disciplines have given much in the way of techniques for diagnosing and treating the learning problems of children. *Educational therapy* is a concept which encompasses the findings of these disciplines, while dedicating itself exclusively to the educational problems of the child who has difficulty learning academic material.

This book is not to be considered a general textbook for use in any one specialized field of education. It is not meant to be a review of the entire literature of related fields. This book, written at the request of our colleagues, is a summary of the principles, methods, and materials which we have used successfully with children who have learning problems. Since this is a handbook, it has been kept as brief as possible and the use of highly specialized terminology has been kept to a minimum.

The central theme of this book is *education*. Many factors touch the life of a child who has a learning problem. But unless a factor is of educational significance, it is not discussed in these pages.

Educational therapy is a new, even a pioneer, field. If you have any suggestions concerning future revisions of this book, please contact us. We are especially interested in hearing your views concerning new problem areas, diagnostic and teaching techniques and materials, and professional publications related to this field.

PATRICK ASHLOCK
115 Walnut Street
Carrollton, Illinois

ALBERTA STEPHEN
2501 45th Street
Galveston, Texas

ACKNOWLEDGMENTS

WE ARE INDEBTED to the following publishers for permitting us to quote from their publications: David McKay Company, Consulting Psychologists Press, Charles E. Merrill Books, and Harper & Row, Publishers.

To the many children, teachers, and parents who have stimulated our thinking, we are sincerely grateful. If it had not been for our relationships with these people, this book would not have been written.

We wish to express our special appreciation to our secretary, Mrs. Eleanor Abrath, and to our readers, Fred Abrath and David Cristao, for the preparation of this manuscript.

P. A.
A. S.

CONTENTS

EDUCATIONAL THERAPY
IN THE
ELEMENTARY SCHOOL

Chapter I

WHAT IS EDUCATIONAL THERAPY?

FOR MANY YEARS, educators have realized that remedial instruction is often necessary. Recently, many new materials and methods have been introduced into this field. Remedial instruction has been effective to various extents, depending upon the intellectual endowment and attitudes of the child and to the effectiveness of the materials, methods, and teachers involved.

In our work, however, we have felt a need for *a new field of education*—one which would set for itself the following goals: describing the child's problems, analyzing his abilities, proposing possible solutions to his problems, building him up for remedial teaching, and helping him move smoothly into remedial instruction. Too often a child is plunged into a remedial situation for which he is unprepared. To help classroom and special teachers, school supervisors, and psychologists working with children, we offer in this book our ideas concerning a frontier area of education: *educational therapy.*

Definition of General Terms

Education: "progressive or desirable changes in a person as a result of teaching and study" (35, p. 169).

Therapy: "treatment intended to cure or alleviate a disordered condition, so that normal functioning is brought about" (35, p. 552).

Educational therapy: The treatment of learning disorders through the application of educational and psychological principles of learning and adjustment. Such treatment is usually

3

used as a prelude to, or in conjunction with, specialized educational techniques and materials employed to diminish the discrepancy between the learner's academic potential and level of attainment.

Aims of Educational Therapy

1. To help the child overcome physical, emotional and intellectual blocks which interfere with the effective learning of academic material.
2. To help the child develop a style of learning.
3. To help the child develop a realistic concept of himself as a learner.
4. To help the child prepare for remedial instruction and to enhance the effectiveness of the early stages of remedial instruction.

Principles of Educational Therapy

1. Human beings are our most valuable resource. As such, the years spent in the elementary school must be as beneficial as possible to both child and society.
2. Children are individuals with free wills. As such, they must assume some responsibility for improving the effectiveness of their learning.
3. Children learn most effectively through a somewhat individualized combination of instructional methods, materials, and personnel.
4. At times, children must learn to subordinate their own styles of learning to a type of instruction designed for the group as a whole.

Characteristics of the Effective Educational Therapist

1. The educational therapist, regardless of whether employed as teacher, psychologist, or under the title of "educational therapist," must be first and last, a skilled *teacher*.
2. It is most advantageous if the children like the educational therapist; it is essential that they respect him.
3. The educational therapist should be, at the appropriate

times, stable, flexible, dependable, consistent and demanding.

4. The educational therapist should be secure and confident—not threatened by the child or his problems.
5. The educational therapist should be able to demonstrate competencies with a variety of educational methods and materials.

What Educational Therapy Is Not

Educational therapy is not, in itself, a cure for the child's learning problem. Rather, educational therapy is a prelude to, a preparation for, and a reinforcement of improved performance.

Chapter II

WHO NEEDS EDUCATIONAL THERAPY?

A child needs educational therapy when his level of academic achievement is significantly below his academic potential, and when he is not able to benefit from remedial instruction alone.

The level of academic achievement can be determined through the use of informal or standardized achievement tests. A discussion of these can be found in Chapter III.

It is not easy to determine a child's academic potential. Too often we obtain an intelligence quotient and say that this represents a child's learning potential. It is a fallacy to do this because the results of an intelligence test only show how certain aspects of the child's intellect have developed to date. The IQ score represents only one facet of a child's academic potential.

At the present time, educational psychologists do not know all the factors which constitute a child's learning potential. Some of those which are known include: level of intellectual functioning as measured by a standardized intelligence test, degree of emotional stability and freedom from emotional conflict, ability to concentrate, level of aspiration, interest in the skill or subject matter to be learned, the personalities involved in the learning situation, the teaching methods used, and the child's particular style of learning. At the present time, only an approximation of a child's learning ability can be made. Thus, the educational therapist (who should be well versed in education, psychology, and child development) should take all of the previously mentioned factors into consideration and approximate the grade level

6

at which the child can be expected to work in the various skill and subject areas after remedial instruction is completed.

It has been stated that a child may need educational therapy if there is a *significant* gap between his academic achievement and potential. What constitutes such a gap? Since a child's learning potential cannot be determined exactly, a child should usually not be given educational therapy if the discrepancy between academic achievement and approximated potential is less than one academic year (ten months). In most cases, a child should not receive educational therapy unless he has spent one full year in grade one.

Too often, we are afraid, educators will use educational therapy only with children who are performing at a level below their grade placement. It should be pointed out that even the gifted child may need educational therapy if he is not working up to his potential. A third grader doing good third grade work may need educational therapy if he is gifted.

On the other hand, not all children working below their grade placement need educational therapy. If it has been determined by a qualified psychologist that a child is mentally retarded, and if that child is working up to his estimated intellectual potential, the child needs special class placement, not educational therapy. But, the retarded child working below his ability level may be in need of such treatment.

The second condition which makes a child a candidate for educational therapy is that he is not able to benefit from remedial education alone. Too often a child is placed in remedial instruction when he is not ready to benefit from it. This is an undesirable thing to do because if an underachiever fails in remedial education, what is there left for him? For the protection of the child's concept of himself as a learner, educators, psychologists, and medical doctors should be careful when they recommend remedial instruction for a child.

What are some of the factors which can make a child unready for remedial education? All of the factors are not known, but some of those now recognized by educational therapists are as follows:

1. *Inadequate motor performance.*

   It should be pointed out that problems caused by lack of maturation are ones over which the educational therapist has no control. But, with the passage of time, the child can usually profit from learning experiences of the type provided by the educational therapist.

2. *Uneven mental ability structure.*

   When a child thinks, he uses a number of different mental skills such as rote memory, abstract thinking, reasoning, visual and auditory memory, association, and creative thinking. These skills are not equally well developed in any one child at any one time. Sometimes the educational therapist must help the child make the best use of his thinking skills.

3. *Deficits in the area of sensory acuity.*

   Children who are having learning problems should, as a matter of routine, be given tests of visual and auditory acuity. If defects are found in these areas, the child should be treated by the appropriate medical specialist before remedial instruction is initiated.

4. *Inadequate perceptual skills.*

   It has been recognized by workers in the field (14, 23, 36, 42, 56, 87, 127, 145, 146) that visual perception is very important in learning. If a child has a visual perceptual problem, he may have 20/20 visual acuity, but the brain may not be correctly interpreting what the eyes have seen.

   The work of Bond (16) and Rose (121) has shown that not only auditory perception, but auditory memory is of great importance in learning. Bond's findings seemed to imply that auditory memory might serve as one means of indicating which children would benefit from different types of reading instruction.

   Benton and his associates (10, 11, 12, 13) have pointed out that poor tactile perception may present learning problems. It was concluded that stereognostic capacity shows growth between the ages of three and six, and may continue to develop past the age of six. Finger localization skill was shown to increase to the age of nine years.

Strauss and Lehtinen (133) and Cruickshank, Bice, and Wallen (26) have treated extensively the learning problems of the brain-injured or neurologically impaired child. The perceptual problems of these children can be especially severe.

In any of these cases, the child will need specialized educational management before he can benefit from remedial instruction alone.

5. *Lack of interest in learning.*

In spite of what we may wish to believe concerning the nature of childhood, there are some children who "just don't give a damn" when it comes to academic learning. Modern theories of motivation are many and complex, but many of them are "carrot" and "pitchfork" theories. (One either gets a mule to move by holding a carrot in front of him or by prodding him with a pitchfork.)

Most children uninterested in learning will require some sugar coating or coercion, or both, to get them going. These children will be more willing to attempt initial learning experiences if such experiences are student oriented, and concerned with student goals. In setting the initial learning goals, the educational therapist should talk *with* the child rather than *to* him. The child will be most interested in goals which will yield him immediate benefit. It is hoped that in the later stages of educational therapy, most children will internalize some form of interest either in the skills they are learning, the subject matter, or the feelings of success they are obtaining.

Of course, it must be admitted that some children could not care less about learning academic skills, no matter what is done with them. In such cases, these children cannot be considered good risks for remedial instruction.

6. *Emotional disturbance.*

If a child is so upset that he can get nothing from remedial instruction, it should be delayed until such a time when he can learn. It is better to spend time on counseling and the care of the child's emotional needs than wasting time on remedial instruction. If the emotional disturbance is not completely disabling, a combination of treatment for the disturbance, educational therapy, and remedial instruction might be worked out.

7. *Inability to concentrate.*

   This condition may be due to low intellectual functioning (78, 79), immaturity (25, 110), lack of sensory acuity (15), brain damage (133), lack of meaningfulness of the learning situation (67), emotional problems (45), high need for body movement (129, 29), lack of self discipline, and physical discomfort.

8. *Having a motive for not learning.*

   Sometimes children do not learn because it is more profitable for them not to. We have seen children who have been receiving so much attention at home because they were "problem children" that they would not give up being "problem children" for the world. In other cases, children have problems because one of the parents (usually the mother) wants them to. We have seen mothers bring children for treatment, only to terminate the therapy at the first signs of progress. In such cases, progress would have destroyed the mothers' much-valued feeling of "martyrdom" which comes from having a child with a learning problem.

9. *The child's lack of a realistic concept of himself as a learner.*

   A child can lack a realistic concept of himself as a learner in two major ways. First, he can so undervalue his abilities that he will not attempt to work up to his expected level of achievement. Second, he will so overestimate (or seem to overestimate) his level of achievement that he will not settle down to work on the "baby" skills that he needs. In either case, the child needs to develop a realistic level of aspiration before going into remedial work. Of course, the complete change of self-concept will come only after remedial work has been satisfactorily completed.

10. *An undeveloped style of learning.*

   All of us have a style of learning, whether we recognize it or not. Efficient learners have worked out (consciously or otherwise) appropriate methods for tackling different types of learning tasks.

Most children with learning problems have not worked out such a method and proceed "hit or miss" (mostly miss) as they approach a learning situation. The educational therapist needs to work out with the child a preliminary or experimental method for learning. This can be modified later as remedial instruction progresses.

If one or more of the above conditions are contributing to a child's learning problem, he is not yet ready to benefit from remedial instruction, or from remedial instruction alone. Educational therapy, with its emphasis upon building up the child and minimizing the contributing problems, is needed in all of these cases.

Chapter III

DESCRIBING THE LEARNING PROBLEM

I N OUR WORK with children who have learning problems, we have become increasingly dissatisfied with the term *diagnosis*. People tend to think that a causal factor must be found for a learning problem. This is not always possible. Also, the causal factor may be overlaid through the years by many other factors. We feel that diagnostic work, where possible, is important—but only a part of describing the learning problem.

Physical Problems

First, let us turn our attention to some possible physical problems that our ineffective learner may have. Over-all physical development, neurological development, coordination, sensory development, and physical fitness are all areas in which learning problems may begin.

We will present a list of possible physical trouble-points. If the child with whom you are working shows a number of these characteristics, further investigation into the physical area may be in order. Remember, these are descriptions, not diagnostic terms.

Some Physical Characteristics of Ineffective Learners

I. Gross motor:
   A. Awkward and clumsy.
   B. Has difficulty skipping, jumping, hopping, and walking backward.
   C. Has difficulty ascending stairs.

D. Has difficulty descending stairs.

E. Has trouble playing games requiring general body balance.

F. Walks with an unusual gait.

G. Often drops things.

H. Has trouble with buttons, snaps, zippers, etc.

I. Does not have a clear concept of his body in space.

J. Has not developed clear concepts of right and left.

II. Physical fitness.

    A. Gets tired easily.

    B. Does not sleep well.

    C. Distractible—cannot sit still, always looking around.

    D. Is winded easily.

    E. Cannot keep up with peers in strenuous activities.

III. Visual acuity.

    A. Squints.

    B. Eyes swollen.

    C. Rubs eyes.

    D. Complains of dizziness.

    E. Complains that he cannot see the blackboard.

    F. Eyes itch.

    G. Says that the words move or jump.

    H. Facial expression appears strained.

    I. Eyes water.

    J. Holds the head to one side or the other while reading.

IV. Auditory acuity.

    A. Seems to watch the teacher's lips.

    B. Does not respond immediately when the speaker is out of the child's range of vision.

    C. Gets similar phonic and phonetic elements confused.

    D. Mispronounces words usually pronounced correctly by peers.

    E. Does not seem to immediately grasp verbal directions.

V. Eye-hand coordination.

    A. Cannot adequately trace a line, circle, or square.

    B. Cannot adequately copy a line, circle, or square.

    C. Has trouble with cutting, folding, and pasting.

D. Has difficulty with juvenile puzzles.

E. Has difficulty coloring predrawn pictures.

The list of characteristics presented is only a list of possible trouble areas. For more formalized study of a child's physical development, we suggest the following:

I. Gross motor.

A. *The Slow Learner in the Classroom* (76).

Primary grades and up.

In this book, Kephart gives the teacher many concrete suggestions for evaluating the gross motor development of the child. The tests have valuable implications for training.

II. Physical fitness.

A. *Kraus-Weber Test* (76, 83, 115).

Preschool through adult.

This test is designed to measure *minimum* physical fitness. There are six subtests in the test, each measuring a different aspect of muscular fitness. Kagerer (73) found that two of the subtests were related to academic achievement in the primary grades.

B. *New York State Physical Fitness Screening Test* (108).

Grades 4 through 12.

This physical fitness test can be used to measure such physical attributes as posture, accuracy, strength, agility, speed, balance, and endurance. An advantage of this test over the Kraus-Weber is that the New York State Physical Fitness goes far beyond the measurement of *minimum* physical fitness. On the other hand, the New York test requires more equipment.

We believe that a child's posture is an important aspect not only of his physical fitness, but of his personality as well. In the New York State Physical Fitness Test, a score is obtained for posture, but because the child is standing in a fixed position, we doubt that a true picture of his postural habits can be thus obtained. Therefore, we suggest that teachers supplement the child's posture score with observations of his posture during his daily activities.

III. Visual acuity.
   A. *Keystone Visual Survey* (91).
   Preschool through adult.

   An instrument called the Telebinocular is used in testing the child's visual acuity, color vision, depth perception, and fusion for both distance and near vision. The Telebinocular is expensive, but when used by someone who is experienced in administering and interpreting this test, it can be one of the best screening tests of vision.
   B. *Signs of Eye Trouble in Children* (126).
   Preschool through adult.

   The National Society for the Prevention of Blindness has put out this small leaflet describing behavior, appearance, and complaints which may indicate eye difficulties in children. The leaflet can be obtained by writing to the Society and requesting Publication 351.

IV. Auditory acuity.
   A. *Whisper Test.*
   Preschool through adult.

   This is a crude test of hearing acuity, and is used only to make the most preliminary evaluation when an audiometer is not available. Hearing in each ear is tested while the other ear is covered with the child's hand. The examiner should first determine how far away the majority of the pupils can hear when he whispers softly and enunciates clearly. The child being examined then stands at least twenty feet away from the examiner, facing so that the child cannot see the examiner's lips. The child repeats each word as he hears it. He moves closer if he does poorly at the average distance.

   By dividing the distance at which the child can hear by the average class distance, the percent of hearing efficiency can be obtained. Thus:

   $$\frac{\text{distance at which child can hear}}{\text{distance at which class can hear}} = \frac{\%\text{ of hearing}}{\text{efficiency}}$$

   B. *Watch Tick Test.*
   Preschool through adult.

   This also is a crude test to be used in the absence of more

refined techniques. The examiner uses a loud ticking watch. The child covers one ear while hearing in the other is being tested. As the watch is moved farther away from the child, he says "yes" or "no" according to whether he can hear it. A yardstick is used to measure the distance at which he can hear. The average class distance for hearing is determined, and each child's performance is compared with this.

C. *Audiometric testing.*

Preschool through adult.

Audiometers are all basically alike. They can be obtained from a number of companies.

1. *Massachusetts Test of Hearing.*

Preschool through adult.

Up to forty children can be screened at one time. The results of this test can be used to separate those with normal hearing from those with questionable hearing. For those who do not pass this test, it is repeated. Those who fail a second time are referred for a Sweep Check Test.

2. *Sweep Check Test.*

Preschool through adult.

One child is tested at a time, one ear at a time, one frequency at a time. The time required for each child is about three minutes. Those who do not pass this test are referred for a Pure Tone Threshold Acuity Test.

3. *Pure Tone Threshold Acuity Test.*

Preschool through adult.

This is called a discreet frequency test. A sound threshold is established for each ear. One child is tested at a time, one ear at a time, one frequency at a time. This test differs from the Sweep Check Test in that one establishes how softly each frequency can be heard. The total test requires about five minutes.

V. Eye-hand coordination.

A. *Bender Motor Gestalt Test* (9) .

Ages four through adult.

This test consists of eight figures which must be copied

by the child, one at a time. There are no time limits. The child's performance can be scored according to how closely his reproductions resemble the original drawings. We use this test for evaluating the eye-hand coordination and visual perception of children, but not as a basis for making clinical judgments. An extensively detailed monograph (8) on the use of the test is available.

Perceptual Problems

Perception is the mental interpretation of the sensations received from stimuli.

Visual perception is the mental interpretation of what the individual sees.

Auditory perception is the mental interpretation of what the individual hears.

Tactile perception is the mental interpretation of what the individual experiences through the sense of touch.

Kinesthetic perception is the mental interpretation of what the individual experiences through the movements of his body.

Appropriate perception has taken place (for our educational purposes) when a child has made a mental interpretation which meets a standard set for his norm group by the society in which he operates. For instance, in our society each letter of the alphabet has only one name, and we expect the "normal" child in the primary grades to learn to call each by its name only.

Inappropriate perception has taken place (for our educational purposes) when a child has made a mental interpretation which does not meet a standard set for his norm group by the society in which he operates. For instance, a school child who recognizes a dog as a horse has made an inappropriate perception.

Our definitions of appropriate and inappropriate perception have both cultural and cognitive implications. Different cultures set different standards for their children. This can be verified by anyone who has tried to give one of our standard intelligence tests to someone from another cultural milieu. Also, we expect that people of different intellectual abilities will differ in the degree of exactness of their perceptions.

Adequate perception is of central importance in the educational process. A perceptual disorder can seriously hamper a child's learning. On the following pages we offer a number of perceptual tests which we have found to be useful in evaluating the perceptual strengths and weaknesses of children.

1. *Marianne Frostig Developmental Test of Visual Perception* (40).

Preschool to grade 4+.

This is a battery of tests of visual perception, but other cognitive aspects are involved as well. The test can be given to children in groups or individually. The battery can be teacher administered. Retraining materials are available for the areas tested. The five sections are described by Frostig (40, p. 11) as follows:

Test I: Eye-Motor Coordination—a test of eye hand coordination involving the drawing of continuous straight, curved, or angled lines between boundaries of various width, or from point to point without guide lines.

Test II: Figure-Ground—a test involving shifts in perception of figures against increasingly complex grounds. Intersecting and 'hidden' geometric forms are used.

Test III: Constancy of Shape—a test involving the recognition of certain geometric figures presented in a variety of sizes, shadings, textures, and position in space, and their discrimination from similar geometric figures. Circles, squares, ellipses and parallelograms are used.

Test IV: Position in Space—a test involving the discrimination of reversals and rotations of figures presented in series. Schematic drawings representing common objects are used.

Test V: Spatial Relationships—a test involving the analysis of simple forms and patterns. These consist of lines of various lengths and angles which the child is required to copy, using dots as guide points.

2. *Examining For Aphasia* (34).

Preschool through adult.

Although this screening instrument was designed for use with adults, we use three sections of it for evaluating difficulties in visual, auditory, and tactile perception. In the visual perception subtest, the child is asked to recognize common objects, pictures, colors, forms, reduced size pictures, numbers, letters, printed words, and printed sentences. In demonstrating the degree of auditory perception, the child is required to recognize sounds and to point to parts of the body named by the examiner. In assessing difficulties in tactile perception, the examiner asks the child to identify common objects by touch. We feel that the use of this instrument is valuable not only for formulating a description of the child's perceptual problems, but also for finding an indication of which sensory avenues should be used in teaching the child.

3. *Illinois Test of Psycholinguistic Abilities* (7, 80, 88–90, 125) . Preschool through grade 4.

The two decoding tests from the ITPA, Auditory Decoding and Visual Decoding, can be used to appraise a child's perception in these two areas. In the test of auditory perception, the child must comprehend spoken words. In the visual perception test, the child must comprehend pictures and written words.

4. *Auditory Discrimination Test* (150) . Primary grades.

The examiner pronounces words in pairs. The child must decide whether the examiner has said the same word twice or two different, but similar, words.

5. *Detroit Tests of Learning Aptitude* (6) . Preschool through adult.

(We have found the sections described below to be of most use in the primary grades, and with children in the intermediate grades who have severe learning problems.)

We have found this entire battery to be excellent in evaluating the intellectual functioning of children. The sections which we use for testing perception are: Auditory Attention Span for Unrelated Words, Visual Attention Span for Objects, Memory for Designs, Auditory Attention Span for Related Syllables, and Visual Attention Span for Letters.

Three of these tests seem to be especially valuable in appraising a youngster's reading potential. In a study by Ashlock (3), it was found that the correlation between reading performance, as measured through the use of the Gates Primary and Advanced Primary Reading Tests (48, 46) and the Visual Attention Span for Letters from the Detroit was +.65. The subjects for the study were ninety children in the primary grades. In the same study, it was found that the correlation between the Memory for Designs test from the Detroit and reading performance was +.54. It was also found that the correlation between reading performance and the Visual Attention Span for Objects from the Detroit was +.47.

6. *Wechsler Intelligence Scale for Children* (149).
Preschool to or through grade 10.

There are four subtests from the WISC which are commonly used in appraising the visual perception of children. These are: Coding, Block Design, Object Assembly, and Picture Completion. Although these subtests measure a number of facets of intellectual performance, all appear to measure some aspect of visual perception.

In the Ashlock study (3) mentioned previously, the following correlations were found between reading performance and these four subtests from the WISC: Coding, +.28, Block Design, +.39, Object Assembly, +.28, Picture Completion, +.09. It is our opinion that when evaluating the visual perception of primary grade children prior to the initiation of remedial reading instruction, the previously mentioned tests from The Detroit Tests of Learning Aptitude offer more information to the educator than do these four subtests from the WISC.

7. *The Ashlock Tests of Visual Perception* (3).
Primary grades.

This battery presently consists of two tests—*Test 1: Word Forms,* and *Test 2: Phrase Forms.* Other tests are to be added to the battery in the future. These two tests can be teacher administered. There are no time limits. While the tests were originally administered to "normal" children, we believe that the instruments can be useful to teachers of the mentally retarded, brain injured, emotionally disturbed, and remedial readers. If the situation requires it, the directions can be given in pantomine. Consequently, the tests can be used for deaf children and children who do not understand, or respond to, spoken English.

Test 1: Word Forms is used to determine whether a child can select one of four word forms which matches the cue word. If the teacher so desires, she may further analyze the child's performance to determine what proportion of his errors are due to inversions, transpositions, or confusions with a similar word form.

Test 2: Phrase Forms is used to evaluate the child's perceptual ability in recognizing phrase-like combinations of letters. The test is so structured that simple letter combinations are attempted by the child first, then he proceeds to increasingly complex phrase-like combinations.

The two tests were administered to one first, one second, and one third grade. An odd-even test of reliability was carried out. The reliability coefficients of Tests 1 and 2 were found to be .64 and .79 respectively. Each item was then analyzed for difficulty by finding what percent of the children passed the item. The items in the tests were then so rearranged that the easiest item appeared at the beginning of the test, and the items then became progressively more difficult.

In the Ashlock study (3) previously mentioned, Tests 1 and 2 were correlated with reading performance. The correlation coefficients between reading performance and Test 1: Word Forms was found to be +.49. The correlation coefficient between reading performance and Test 2: Phrase Forms was found to be +.58.

8. *Tests of Tactile and Kinesthetic Ability.*
Preschool to or through intermediate grades.

Benton and his associates have produced four publications in this area which we believe to be of value (10, 11, 12, 13).

Language Problems

1. *Illinois Test of Psycholinguistic Abilities* (7, 80, 88, 89, 90, 125).
   Preschool to or through grade 4.

   The Decoding Tests of the ITPA have been described in the section on perception. The association tests, Test III: Auditory-Vocal Association and Test IV: Visual-Motor Association, are concerned with the child's ability to meaningfully use visual and auditory symbols. The encoding tests, Test V: Vocal Encoding and Test VI: Motor Encoding are concerned with the child's ability to express himself in words and gestures. The tests at the automatic-sequential level, Test VII: Auditory-Vocal Automatic, Test VIII: Auditory-Vocal Sequencing, and Test IX: Visual-Motor Sequencing, are concerned with the ability to use nonmeaningful symbols and with the child's ability to remember symbols and symbol sequences for differing lengths of time.

2. *Examining for Aphasia* (34).
   Primary grades through adult.

   We have found parts of this instrument to be of particular value in the appraisal of a child's language performance. The form provides guidance for the examiner in his investigation of the ideational content and level of language functioning. The parts of the instrument which we use for this purpose are the sections on the aphasias and the apraxias.

3. *Robbins Speech Sound Discrimination and Verbal Imagery Tests* (119).
   Preschool through elementary grades.

   This diagnostic and training program is one which should be of great interest to the educational therapist. We have been especially impressed by the author's brief, but concise, description of teaching "eye-minded," "motor-minded," and "ear-minded" children.

4. *Webster Speech Correction Guide* (148).
   Elementary grades.

   This is a one page fold-out chart which we have found useful in dealing with children who have simple articulation difficulties. The chart lists the speech sound, provides a simple basic test for the sound; lists additional test words and test sentences; provides words to be used in checking the sound in blending combinations and endings; gives examples of common speech problems; lists possible corrective measures to be taken; suggests a speech program for an entire class.

Problems of Intellectual Functioning

For a really thorough evaluation of the intellectual functioning of a child with a learning problem, we recommend the following:
1. *Wechsler Intelligence Scale for Children* (149).
   Preschool to or through grade 10.

When a qualified psychological examiner uses this test, he obtains not only a Verbal Intelligence Quotient, a Performance Intelligence Quotient, and a Full Scale Intelligence Quotient, but relative measures of performance on the following types of tasks: general information, general comprehension, arithmetical reasoning, analogies and/or similarities, vocabulary, picture completion, picture arrangement, block design, object assembly, and coding. Two subtests are optional, but usually of interest to the educational therapist: memory for digits (forward and backward) and mazes.

Since the results of the Wechsler may be used by persons who are not qualified psychological examiners, we list below a number of questions which the educational therapist or the teacher may wish to put to the psychologist. Whenever possible, these questions should be submitted to the psychologist *before* he examines the child.

1. How good is this child's auditory memory?
2. How good is this child's visual perception?
3. Can you give any specific causes of this child's learning problem?
4. Is this child's ability to think logically normal for his age?
5. Is this child's ability to think abstractly normal for his age?

6. Is this child's eye-hand coordination normal for his age?
7. In general, what are this child's intellectual strengths and weaknesses?
8. Do you feel that during the testing the child was motivated to do his best?
9. Did the child show anxiety during the test?
10. How good is this child's ability to learn new material?
11. How well does this child work under time pressure?
12. Do you think this child has enough social intelligence to operate adequately with his peers?
13. How would you describe the degree of exactness that this child uses in his verbal expression?
14. In taking the test, did the child stick with it when the tasks became difficult, or did he give up easily?
15. Could this child perceive when a task was successfully completed?
16. How good was this child's ability to follow directions?
17. Do you suspect an emotional problem?
18. Do you suspect cultural or environmental deprivation?
19. Would you say that this child's learning problem is related primarily to his perceptual, associative, or expressive processes?
20. We do not expect you to make our educational plans for us, but what advice can you give us concerning the level of academic performance we can expect from this child in the future?

2. *Stanford-Binet Intelligence Scale* (138).
Preschool to adult.

This scale must be administered by a qualified psychological examiner. Both an intelligence quotient and a mental age can be obtained. This test is especially good for children in the primary grades who are suspected of having mental retardation. Experience has shown that this instrument is a fairly good predictor of academic success or failure.

If the educational therapist is not a qualified psychological examiner, and still wishes to administer his own intelligence test, one of the following might be used:

1. *Non-Language Multi-Mental Test* (137).
Preschool to adult.

This intelligence test measures primarily the ability to educe relationships among pictorial symbols. The test, which can be administered either through the use of verbal directions or pantomime, is useful when evaluating the intelligence of the deaf, the illiterate, the person with a foreign language background, or the child with an expressive difficulty.

2. *The Peabody Picture Vocabulary Test* (33).
Preschool through senior high.

This is an individual intelligence test in which the subject indicates one of four pictures which best matches the stimulus word pronounced by the examiner. Educational therapists dealing with children who have expressive difficulties, cerebral palsy, emotional disturbance, mental retardation, and reading difficulties may find this test to be useful.

3. *California Short-Form Test of Mental Maturity* (135).
Preschool through adult.

This is a shortened adaption of the *California Test of Mental Maturity* (134). The group test is designed to measure four statistically-derived factors: logical reasoning, numerical reasoning, verbal concepts, and memory. A separate mental age and intelligence quotient can be derived for each of the two major subsections: language and nonlanguage. A total IQ and mental age can be derived for the total test.

4. *Goodenough Intelligence Test* (57).
Preschool through the primary grades.

This is the classic draw-a-man test.

5. *SRA Primary Mental Abilities* (144).
Grades kindergarten to 12.

The form of this test to be given to children between the ages of five and seven measures five abilities selected on the basis of a multiple-factor analysis of intelligence. These factors are verbal meaning, perception (perceptual speed), quantitative, motor (coordination of hand and eye movements), and space. The test to be given to children between seven and eleven years of age tests the following five factors: verbal meaning, space, reasoning, perception (perceptual speed) and number.

We recommend these tests for the child who appears to be good in some areas and poor in others because the results of the test show the child's profile of intellectual development.

6. *Otis Quick-Scoring Mental Ability Tests* (112).
   Grades 1 to 5.

   This test has two forms suitable for the elementary grades. The Alpha Test is for grades 1.5 to four. The Beta Test is for grades four to nine. A mental age and an Alpha IQ or Beta IQ can be derived.

   We recommend this for a screening test to determine if an individual intelligence test should be administered.

7. *Series of Emergency Scales* (75).
   Preschool through junior high.

   This is a very informal mental test which can be given when the examiner needs a quick estimate of the child's intellectual functioning. Primarily, the questions on the test refer to the everyday experiences of children.

8. *Detroit Tests of Learning Aptitude* (6).
   Preschool through adult.

   The subtests of this individual intelligence test are: pictorial absurdities, verbal absurdities, pictorial opposites, verbal opposites, motor speed, auditory attention span for unrelated words, oral commissions, social adjustment, visual attention span for objects, orientation, free association, designs, auditory attention span for related syllables, number ability, visual attention span for letters, disarranged pictures, oral directions, and likenesses and differences. Not all of the subtests are to be administered to all individuals at all ages. The construction of the test allows the examiner some measure of flexibility in the selection of the subtests to be administered to the child.

9. *SRA Tests of Educational Ability* (143).
   Grades 4 through 12.

   These tests are designed to be used in assessing a child's potentiality for academic work. Two scores can be obtained as a result of an administration of this test. The total score is more valuable when no reading problem exists. The nonreading total score is a more fair estimate of the intelligence of a child who has a reading problem.

10. *Cattell Culture Fair Intelligence Test* (22).
Age eight through adult.

This test is so structured that school achievement and other influences of the environment are supposed to have a minimal influence on the results.

Problems of Personality Development

For guidance in describing the personality of the child with whom you are working, we suggest these instruments which do not have to be administered by a clinical psychologist.

1. *A Book About Me* (70).
Kindergarten.

While this workbook is of great use to the kindergarten teacher, we have found it to be a valuable device for making an informal evaluation of young retarded, neurologically impaired, and emotionally disturbed children. Typical topics are: "Things I Do At Home," "Things I Can Do All By Myself," "People I See, Know, Like," "Things I Am Afraid Of," and "My Playmates."

2. *California Test of Personality* (140).
Kindergarten through adult.

By administering this test to the child, the examiner can obtain scores on the following personality factors: self-reliance, sense of personal worth, sense of personal freedom, feeling of belonging, withdrawal tendencies, nervous symptoms, total personal adjustment, social standards, social skills, antisocial tendencies, family relations, school relations or occupational relations, community relations, total social adjustment, and total adjustment. As when administering other tests of this type, when the child has a reading problem, the examiner should read the questions to him.

3. *Institute of Child Study Security Test* (58).
Grades 4 through 8.

This instrument is to be used in evaluating the child's feelings of security. The test is in the form of "The Story of Jimmy." It is assumed that the child identifies with Jimmy in answering the questions. Jimmy has relationships with family, peers, and school. He plays and has interests outside of school. He is developing a self-concept and an attitude toward life. We believe that the organization of this test is clever and attractive to children, although it probably appeals more to boys than to girls.

4. *SRA Junior Inventory* (118).

   Grades 4 through 8.

   This questionaire deals with the following categories: "About Me and My School," "About Me and My Home," "About Myself," "Getting Along With Other People," and "Things in General." If the child has any special problems, there is a place for him to record them.

5. *What I Like to Do* (142).

   Grades 4 through 7.

   This questionaire is simply an inventory of children's interests. We have found this to be a good "ice-breaker" when getting acquainted with a child.

A book which has stimulated our thinking in the area of personality problems is *The Early Identification of Emotionally Handicapped Children in School* (19). The author suggests a number of ways these children can be identified and helped.

To further help the educational therapist write a description of the personality of a child with a learning problem, the following list of descriptive terms is provided:

1. Active—passive.
2. Aggressive—withdrawn.
3. Anxious—relaxed.
4. Moral—immoral—amoral.
5. Confident—defensive—feelings of inferiority.
6. Kind—sadistic—masochistic.
7. Happy—unhappy.
8. Emotional—unresponsive.
9. Tense—relaxed.
10. Consistent behavior—inconsistent behavior.
11. Purposeful activity—unpurposeful activity.
12. Introvert—extrovert.
13. Outer directed—self directed—ambivalent.

14. Expressive—undemonstrative.
15. Sensitive to needs and feelings of others—insensitive to the needs and feelings of others.
16. Quarrels and/or fights with peers.
17. Ignores peers.
18. Is ignored by peers.
19. Complains that peer group does not like him, makes fun of him, is not fair, or does not play good games.
20. Prefers to play with much younger children.

Problems of Academic Achievement

An appraisal of a child's levels of academic achievement is important in determining whether a child needs educational therapy and/or remedial instruction. For such an appraisal, we recommend the following instruments:

1. *Harrison-Stroud Reading Readiness Tests** (66).
   Preschool and grade 1.

   This instrument can be used in measuring the child's ability to make visual discriminations, make use of the context, make auditory discriminations, use context and auditory clues, and deal with symbols. Because of the excellent format, we use this test with brain-injured children and children who have visual perceptual handicaps.

2. *American School Reading Readiness Tests* (153).
   Preschool and grade 1.

   This readiness test can be used in assessing the child's level of performance in the following areas: vocabulary, discrimination of letter forms, discrimination of letter combinations, selection of words, matching of words, discrimination of geometric forms, ability to follow directions, and memory of geometric forms.

3. *Scholastic Reading Readiness Test* (1).
   Preschool and grade 1.

* *Note on the diagnostic use of readiness tests:* Readiness tests should not usually be administered to youngsters who have had more than six months of formal schooling. However, we make use of readiness tests as diagnostic instruments for older children who have learning problems. We are not interested in the *scores* that these children make on readiness tests, but in their *style* of performance.

We use Tests 3 and 4 of this instrument for evaluating visual perception and Tests 5 and 6 for measuring auditory perception.

4. *Lee-Clark Reading Readiness Tests* (84).

Preschool and grade 1.

We have found Tests 1, 2, and 4 to be valuable tools in the diagnosis of visual perceptual problems.

5. *Gates Reading Readiness Tests* (44).

Preschool and grade 1.

Separate scores can be obtained for following directions, dealing with pictures, word matching, word-card matching, rhyming, and naming letters and numbers.

6. *Murphy-Durrell Diagnostic Reading Readiness Test* (107).

Preschool and grade 1.

Separate scores can be obtained for auditory perception, visual perception, and learning rate.

7. *Reading Readiness Test* (147).

Preschool and grade 1.

This test is divided into the following sections:

    Familiarity with Names of Objects

    Functions of Objects

    Interpretations of Spoken Sentences

    Differentiation of Pictures and Designs

    Differentiation of Letters

    Differentiation of Pairs of Letters

    Differentiation of Phrases

    Recognition of Patterns

    Recognition of Words

In our opinion, this is an excellent readiness test and diagnostic tool.

8. *Group Test of Reading Readiness: The Dominion Tests* (63).

Preschool and grade 1.

We make use of the sections dealing with visual perception and copying ability.

9. *Wide Range Achievement Test* (69).

Preschool through adult.

This test is to be used only as a preliminary survey of the

child's achievement in the areas of oral reading, spelling, and arithmetic.

10. *SRA Achievement Series* (141).
    Grades 1 through 9.
    The achievement battery for grades one to two consists of separate tests for arithmetic and reading. The battery for grades two to four consists of separate tests for reading, arithmetic, and language. The achievement series for grades four to six includes tests for work-study skills, reading, language arts, and arithmetic.

11. *Stanford Achievement Test (1953 Revision)* (74).
    Grades 1.9 to 9.
    The Primary Battery (grades 1.9 to 3.5) yields scores on paragraph meaning, word meaning, spelling, arithmetic reasoning, arithmetic computation, and a total score. The Elementary Battery (grades three and four) yields scores the same as the Primary Battery plus language. The Intermediate Battery (grades five and six) includes a Complete Battery which is the same as the Elementary Battery plus social studies, science, and study skills and a Partial Battery which is the same as the Elementary Battery.

12. *Iowa Tests of Basic Skills* (85).
    Grades 3 through 9.
    This test is not an achievement battery in the sense of measuring knowledge in the content areas such as social studies, and geography. This test is concerned with the evaluation of the generalized intellectual skills and abilities involved in vocabulary, reading comprehension, language, work-study skills and arithmetic.

13. *Gilmore Oral Reading Paragraphs* (55).
    Grades 1 through 8.
    In administering this test, the examiner asks the child to read graded paragraphs of increasing difficulty. The examiner records the errors made by the child, and classifies them according to the following categories: substitutions, mispronunciations, words pronounced by the examiner, disregard of punctuation, insertions, hesitations, repetitions, and omissions. Five comprehension questions follow each

paragraph. The test has the advantage of coming in two equivalent forms.

14. *Gray Oral Reading Paragraphs* (60).

Grades 1 to 8.

The child reads graded paragraphs of increasing difficulty and the teacher records the errors. A grade score can be obtained. No provision is made for testing the child's reading comprehension.

15. *Measuring Scale for Handwriting: Gettysburg Edition* (5).

Grades 5 through 8.

This scale provides standards for evaluating the quality and rate of cursive writing.

16. *Gates Reading Tests.*

A. *Gates Primary Reading Tests* (48).

Grades 1 to 2.5.

1. *Word Recognition.* The child looks at a picture and selects one of four words which goes with the picture.

2. *Sentence Reading.* The child carries out paper and pencil activities to show his degree of comprehension when reading single sentences.

3. *Paragraph Reading.* The child carries out paper and pencil activities to show his degree of comprehension when reading single paragraphs.

B. *Gates Advanced Primary Reading Test* (46).

Grades 2.5 through 3.

1. *Word Recognition.* The child looks at a picture and selects one of four words which goes with the picture.

2. *Paragraph Reading.* The child carries out paper and pencil activities to show his degree of comprehension when reading single paragraphs.

C. *Gates Reading Survey* (49).

Grades 3.5 through 10.

1. *Speed and Accuracy Test.* This test yields a speed score and a percent of accuracy of comprehension score.

2. *Reading Vocabulary Test.* This untimed test yields a score for the level of reading vocabulary development.

3. *Level of Comprehension Test.* This untimed test yields a score for the accuracy of paragraph comprehension.

D. *Gates Basic Reading Tests* (47).
Grades 3.5 through 8.

1. *Reading for General Significance.* This test measures the child's ability to comprehend the general ideas contained in the reading selections. Timed.

2. *Reading to Understand Precise Directions.* The child carries out precise directions to show that he has understood the material which he has read. Timed.

3. *Reading to Note Details.* The child is required to answer questions which relate to specific details in the reading selection. Timed.

4. *Level of Comprehension.* This is a test of general reading comprehension. Untimed.

5. *Reading Vocabulary.* This is a test of general reading vocabulary. Untimed.

All of the Gates Reading Tests are available in three alternate forms, making a complete and flexible unit.

Descriptive Analysis of Academic Difficulties

Most of these tests are useful because they can be used to give detailed descriptions of the educational aspects of a problem. Some of this information is of interest to the educational therapist; most of it will be used later by the remedial teacher.

1. *Spelling Errors Test* (128).
Grades 2 through 8.

This test is so constructed that the child's performance will indicate what types of spelling errors he is making.

2. *Phonovisual Diagnostic Spelling Test* (124).
Grades 3+.

This test can be used to analyze difficulties the child is having with any of the consonant sounds and seventeen vowel sounds. The test is short, easy to administer, and the results are meaningful in terms of remedial work.

3. *Roswell-Chall Diagnostic Test of Word Analysis Skills* (122).

Grades 2 through 6.

This test is divided into six subtests: single consonants, consonant combinations, short vowels, rule of silent *e*, vowel combinations, and syllabication. The test is available in two forms.

4. *Gates-McKillop Reading Diagnostic Tests* (51).

All grades.

This test is to be administered to one child at a time. It is an excellent instrument for use in the analysis of specific reading problems.

5. *Diagnostic Tests and Self-Helps in Arithmetic* (20).

Grades 1 through 9.

These tests are divided into two major sections. Screening Tests deal with whole numbers, fractions, decimals, and general arithmetic. Diagnostic Tests deal with addition, subtraction, multiplication and division facts, uneven division facts, operations with whole numbers, division by one and two place numbers, operations with fractions, operations with decimals, percentage, and operations with measures. When difficulties are found, appropriate exercises are provided for the use of the educational therapist and/or remedial instructor.

The General Approach

For the educational therapist interested in materials of a more general nature, we suggest the following.

1. *Pupil Adjustment Inventory* (62).

Elementary grades.

This inventory comes in both a long and a short form. The examiner rates the child on various aspects of his development. We have found the long form to be useful in profiling the overall development of a youngster. The major categories of characteristics are: academic, social, emotional, physical activities and interests, school influence upon pupil, and home background.

2. *Studying the Individual Pupil* (151).

All grade levels.

This is an excellent guide to writing an overall description of a child's development.

Guide Lines for Describing the Learning Problem

We suggest the following guide lines for writing a report describing the learning problems of a child:

1. Write the report in narrative style, as far as this is possible.
2. Do not include just *any information*, no matter how interesting, unless it has a direct bearing upon the problem at hand.
3. Be brief.
4. Write in *English* rather than "psychologese" or "pedagese."
5. Use qualifying terms such as:
    "It *appears* that this child. . . ."
    "The problem *seems* to be due primarily to. . . ."
    "One *might* conclude that. . . ."
    "It is *possible* that. . . ."
    "This would *seem* to suggest. . . ."
6. If you suspect something, but cannot prove it—say just that.
7. Think in terms of possible solutions, even when you are not making recommendations at that time.
8. Let the child in on your findings. Show him a rough draft of your report. Ask what he thinks about your findings.
9. Incorporate his reactions into your final report.
10. Relate the findings of contributing disciplines such as speech and hearing, psychology, and medicine to the more central findings of educational diagnosis.

Chapter IV

THE GENERAL PHYSICAL BUILD-UP

IN EDUCATING CHILDREN who have learning problems, we have too often thought in terms of the intellectual *and* physical sides of education. Or worse, we have thought only of the intellectual aspect of such teaching.

The mind is educated through the body. Not only are the senses of sight and hearing important, but also the tactile and kinesthetic senses. The intellect develops through the education of the body. Kephart (76, p. 37) has stated: "There is evidence that the efficiency of the higher thought processes can be no better than the basic motor abilities upon which they are based."

For an excellent description of the relation between physical development and the perceptual skill of school children, we refer the reader to *The Slowlearner in the Classroom* by Newell C. Kephart (76). Kephart's book is divided into three parts: part one deals with the relation between physical development and school achievement; part two deals with a perceptual survey rating scale which we feel is very good; part three is concerned with training activities which we believe to be effective with young children.

Delacato has written two books, *The Treatment and Prevention of Reading Problems* (30) and *The Diagnosis and Treatment of Speech and Reading Problems* (31), which deal with the neurophysiological treatment of learning problems.

Primarily, we are concerned in this chapter with general physical development. How can improved physical fitness help the child who has a learning problem? We hypothesize that a physical fitness and recreational program can aid the child who has an academic learning problem in one or more of the following ways:

1. Increased self-confidence.
2. Increased perseverance.
3. Increased realization of the necessity for practice.
4. Decreased tiredness or fatigue.
5. Decreased tension.
6. Improved gross motor coordination.
7. Improved eye-hand coordination.
8. Improved self-discipline.
9. Decreased distractibility.
10. Improved concepts of position and movement in space.

We have found that the Kraus-Weber Test is one of the most valuable instruments in this field. This instrument consists of six simple tests which can be used to measure minimum physical fitness. Kraus and Hirschland (83) have written a detailed description of this test. Kagerer (73) found that tests 4 and 5 were highly related to school achievement in the early grades. Kephart (76) describes the Kraus-Weber Test and gives techniques for improving the child's physical status. Prudden (115) has written a book in which she gives detailed descriptions of the test, and in which she proposes exercises for improving the child's physical fitness.

For a more general plan of physical activities, we recommend the following:

Complete Book of Games and Stunts (68).
Counseling in the Physical Education Program (21).
Fitness for Elementary School Children Through Physical Education (27).

Instruction in the Motor Functions Basic to Performance in the Skill Subjects

It has often been thought that the basic skill subjects are dependent only upon intellectual development. The educational therapist and the teacher need to be reminded of the motor basis of the skill subjects. We are offering here a list of activities which can be used in strengthening the child's motor functioning, and thus indirectly influencing the outcome of later remedial instruction. Instruction in motor functioning should take place only after the medical doctor has examined for, and corrected, any physical defects as far as possible.

  I. The Visual Function.

    A. Focusing.

        1. *Magnifying glass.* The use of a magnifying glass can increase the child's visual attention span and also his ability to focus upon an object. Most children enjoy using a magnifying glass, and will soon bring all sorts of objects to the therapy session for the purpose of examining them more closely.

        2. *Toy telescope.* The use of a toy telescope can increase a child's ability to focus upon selected objects. Instruction should begin indoors, and after skill in focusing has begun to develop, the sessions can move outdoors for long distance focusing.

        3. *Window card.* A slit can be cut in an index card of the appropriate size. This device is then passed over the printed material that the child is reading. It can be used to block out all the printed matter except for the small area which the child is reading.

        4. *Index cards.* The child may improve his focusing ability by holding an index card so that it blocks out most of the material which he has already read, or, he may wish to use the card to block out most of the material which he has not yet read .

        5. *Projectors.* Any projector used in a darkened, or semi-darkened, room can aid the child in focusing.

        6. *Blinders.* These are made by attaching pieces of cardboard to the arms of a pair of eyeglass frames. These are used to limit the child's field of vision and to direct his attention to the material in front of him.

        7. *Reconstructed learning materials.*

          a. *Reading.* Sometimes it helps a child to focus if the desired portion of reading material is cut out of the page and pasted on a larger sheet of dark paper. If the pictures are found to be disturbing the child instead of aiding his comprehension, the pictures can be removed when the material is being reconstructed.

b. *Arithmetic.* The child may find it easier to focus if the teacher takes a crayon and separately boxes in each item. The teacher may also cut out each problem and mount it separately on a dark piece of paper.

c. *Spelling.* We have found that it helps a child to concentrate upon spelling words if the teacher will underline that part of the word which is giving the child trouble, or underline each syllable of the word.

8. *Kinesthetic reinforcement.* The child may find it easier to focus if he reinforces his focusing by pointing to each word or letter with his finger, or by working aloud.

9. *Lighting.* Focusing is made easier if a right handed child has the light coming over the left shoulder and if a left handed child has the light coming over the right shoulder.

10. *Tasks which require focusing upon details.* We have found that it is beneficial to guide a child to focus upon selected details in pictorial material. Almost any type of pictorial material is suitable for this. Simply ask the child, "In this picture can you pick out _____?"

B. Left to right directionality.

1. *Comic strips.* When reading comic strips to a child with a learning problem, point to the pictures with your hand so the child notices the left to right progression of the story.

2. *Readiness books.* Most readiness books have sets of story pictures which can be used to help the child develop his concept of left to right movement.

3. *Colored boxes.* If the instructor is sure that the child knows his colors, the instructor may draw a series of rows of boxes, coloring each a different color. The

child is then told, "Start here (indicating the left box in the top row) and tell me the colors in the boxes." The instructor also helps the child make the correct return sweep so that he starts in the correct box in the following row.

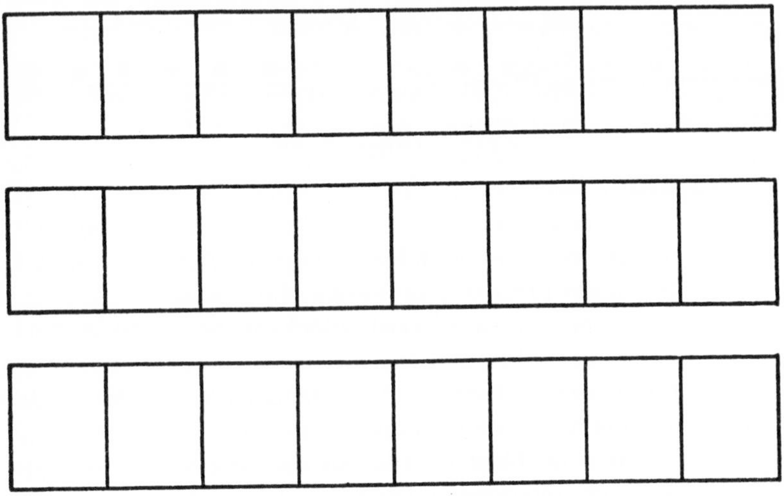

Figure 1. Colored boxes.

4. *Tactile boxes.* The same thing may be done by gluing a different kind of tactile material in each box. For instance, one box can be made of corduroy, the next of plastic, the next of sandpaper. The child proceeds from one box to the next in a left to right direction, telling the teacher how each box feels.

5. *Gripper board.* On a piece of plywood eighteen inches long and six inches wide, tack a piece of cloth the same length to the top of the board. On the bottom of the board, attach a strip of cloth with a gripper tape sewn on. Fold up two inches and snap to the top cloth which has the other half of the gripper sewn in the bottom of it. The child unfastens the grippers in a left to right direction. As an added motivation, the educational therapist may place a different picture under the cloth each time so that the child will have some purpose for his activity.

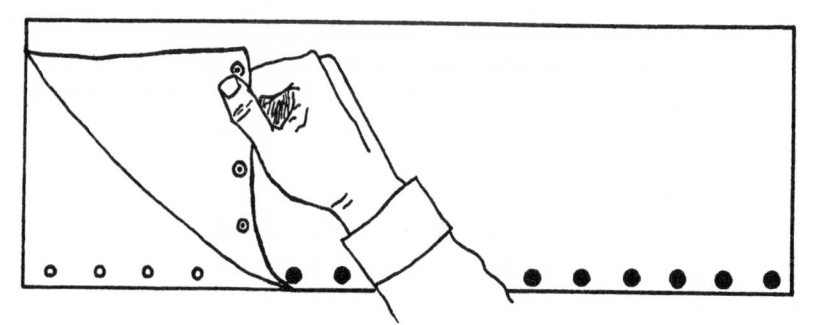

Figure 2. Gripper board.

C. Return sweep.

For success in reading, the child must learn not only left to right eye movement, but also the return sweep from the end of one line to the beginning of the next.

The primary word card holder can be placed in front of the child. He is given picture cards and told to line them up in rows. In so doing, he is using both the left to right and the return sweep movements.

Harris, in *How To Increase Reading Ability* (64, pp. 521–524) offers a number of good suggestions on how to overcome difficulty in making the return sweep.

II. The Auditory Function.

A. Listening.

We must realize that even if the child can hear, he might not have learned to listen. Listening to nursery rhymes, stories, records, verbal directions, comparing sounds for loudness and softness, and identifying sources of sounds are useful.

B. Auditory-verbal matching.

An important aspect of auditory skill is that of verbally reacting to the world of sound. Activities in this area include learning to repeat nursery rhymes, learning to complete nursery rhymes begun by the teacher, learning to imitate the sounds of animals, and to adjust the loudness of one's speech so that it is appropriate for the distance between one and the person to whom one is talking.

III. The Eye-Hand Coordination Function.

Eye-hand coordination is not only important because of the

way in which the hand can be used to reinforce visual performance, but because many of the seat work and workbook activities which are supplementary to basic reading instruction are heavily dependent upon eye-hand coordination.

A. Puzzles.

Many commercial puzzles are available for this type of activity. Or, the teacher may wish to make puzzles out of pictorial material which is especially meaningful to the child being taught.

B. Lock box.

The lock box consists of a box filled with padlocks of various sizes to which the keys are attached by means of long chains. By locking and unlocking the locks, the child develops eye-hand coordination and manual dexterity.

C. Folding, cutting, and pasting activities.

1. For folding activities, both paper and cloth should be used.
2. Cutting activities should be as purposeful as possible.
3. Pasting activities such as adhering a precut pattern to a predrawn outline are especially good for this type of training.

D. Tracing.

We use dime store tracing materials, such as workbooks in which onion skin covers a drawing, and the child traces the drawing on the thin covering.

E. Coloring.

Duplicate pictures, one of which is colored, and the other not colored, have been found to be useful in developing eye-hand coordination.

IV. The Body-Language Function.

The child's initial language concepts are based on the experiences he has with his own body. Training in this area is basic to conceptualization. We use the following organizational pattern when we try to teach the *stages in the development of thinking skills.*

A. *Passive-experiential Stage.*

At this stage, experiences are provided *for* the child. He is taken on field trips, read to, sung to, told stories, shown pictures, played with, talked to, etc. At this stage, the child's learning is primarily concerned with the *intake* of concepts.

B. *Active-experiential Stage.*

At this stage, the child is encouraged to *engage in* a number of varied experiences. He acquires a pet, plants a garden, makes short trips of his own, constructs some of his own playthings, makes up games, etc.

C. *Perceptual-experiential Stage.*

At this stage, the adult guides the child's perceptual learnings. To develop *auditory perception,* the adult calls the child's attention to the loudness or softness of sounds, the differences in people's voices, the word sequence in simple songs, rhyming, etc. To develop *tactile-kinesthetic perception,* the adult calls the child's attention to objects that are cold, wet, soft, sticky, sharp, hard, slippery, hot, etc. To develop *visual perception,* the adult calls the child's attention to likenesses and differences in shapes of objects, the sizes of objects, the nearness and distance of things, etc.

D. *Image-formulation Stage.*

At this level, the adult calls the child's attention to the many attributes of objects and to the spatial and temporal aspects of things. The meanings of such words as red, green, blue, large, small, soft, hard, tall, short, on, in, out, beside, over, under, late, early, doing, jumping, sleeping, playing, etc. are developed at this time.

E. *Category-formulation Stage.*

At this stage, the adult helps the child conceptualize in terms of the classification or taxonomy of things. For instance, the child is encouraged to think in terms of things to ride in, toys, flowers, vegetables, animals, places, games, numerical groupings, etc.

F. *Relational-conceptual Stage.*

At this stage, the child is guided to think in terms of cause and effect and of sequential progression of events. Cause and effect conceptualizations involve the answering of such questions as "'Why did this happen?" "Why is this

so?" and "If I do this, what will happen?" Conceptualization of sequential progression of events involves helping
the child think in terms of time.

G. *Creative-conceptual Stage.*

At this stage, the adult stimulates the child to pull together past concepts and manipulate them so that a newly
organized concept evolves. This is probably the highest
stage in the development of thinking skills.

Chapter V

THE SENSORY AND PERCEPTUAL
BUILD-UP

WE HAVE FOUND that many of our pupils in need of remedial instruction have benefitted from a preliminary period of sensory and perceptual training. In this way we have sought to build up our children's learning powers before placing them under remedial instruction.

The idea of sensory and perceptual training is not new. The work of Montessori (24, 37, 38, 71, 93, 94, 95, 96, 97, 98, 99, 100, 101, 102, 103, 104, 105, 106, 130, 131) is well known. All educational therapists should be acquainted with Montessori's methods. Rambush (117) has written a readable account of her work with the Montessori method in this country. Rambush's book is appropriately titled, *Learning How to Learn,* and subtitled, "An American Approach to Montessori."

Again, we call attention to Kephart's work, *The Slow Learner in the Classroom* (76). In this volume are found many hints on how to improve perceptual performance. A somewhat more readable account of Kephart's methods can be found in *Success Through Play* (116) by Radler and Kephart.

Jolles (72) has suggested "A Teaching Sequence for the Training of Visual and Motor Perception." The reader is referred to this source for a concise set of suggestions for training in this area.

We suggest the following principles for sensory-perceptual training. Each principle is illustrated in Table I by pointing out how the principle would be followed in teaching the alphabet letters to a child who has severe learning difficulties.

TABLE I

LEVELS OF SENSORY-PERCEPTUAL TRAINING

Levels of Sensory-Perceptual Training	Example: The teaching of alphabetic symbols to a child who has severe learning difficulties
1. *Auditory perception of dissimilar sounds.* The child learns to perceive and differentiate among dissimilar sounds.	The child is given three or four letter names and asked to select the one that is different. If the child is unable to do this, work with pairs of words such *pin* and *pen*, *sit* and *sit*, *pick* and *sick*, asking the child to say whether the two words are alike or different. If this task is too difficult for the child, begin training again with gross sounds such as clapping, tapping, whistling, etc. Ask the child to tell you if the sounds you are making are alike or different. When learning is solidly successful at a level, begin working up the scale until the child can perceive and differentiate among dissimilar letter names.
2. *Auditory perception of similar sounds.* The child learns to perceive and match similar sounds.	The child is given three or four letter names, two of which are the same. He is expected to select the two that are the same.
3. *Passive kinesthetic-tactile.* The teacher guides the child through muscle movements and touch experiences which will form a basis for later perceptual experiences of a higher order.	The teacher takes the child's dominant hand and moves it over large alphabet letters so that the tip of the index finger traces each letter. The teacher maintains correct directionality at all times.
4. *Active kinesthetic-tactile.* The child uses the senses of touch and muscle movement to perform the acts taught to him at Level 3. The teacher supervises, but does not actually move the child's hand.	The teacher gives the large alphabet letters to the child and he traces them, using correct directionality. The teacher interferes only if the child makes a mistake.
5. *Passive kinesthetic-tactile.* This is the same as Level 3, except that the sense of touch is no longer used. The tracing is now done with a pencil, crayon, pen, felt point pen, etc.	The child, with the help of the teacher, traces the letters with a pencil or similar instrument. If Levels 3 and 4 have been successfully passed, a minimum of time will need to be spent on Level 5.
6. *Active kinesthetic.* This is the same as Level 4, except that the sense of touch is not used. The tracing is done with a pencil or similar instrument.	The child, without the manual guidance of the teacher, traces each letter with a pencil or similar instrument. The teacher interferes only if the child makes a mistake.
7. *Visual perception of dissimilar symbols.* At this level, the child learns to perceive and differentiate among dissimilar visual symbols.	The child is given four letter forms, three of which are alike, and is taught to select the one that is different.
8. *Visual perception of similar symbols.* The child learns to perceive and recognize the similarity of visual symbols.	The child is given one letter form and from three or four letter forms must select the one that matches the one given to him.

Levels of Sensory-Perceptual Training	Example: The teaching of alphabetic symbols to a child who has severe learning difficulties
9. *Visual perception and kinesthetic reproduction.* At this level the child learns to perceive visual symbols and kinesthetically reproduce them.	The child looks at the letter given to him and copies it with a pencil or other instrument.
10. *Visual-auditory association.* The child learns to associate visual symbols with their names.	The child is shown a letter and told its name. He is trained until he automatically says the letter name when it is shown to him.
11. *Auditory-visual association.* The child learns to associate letter names and their visual symbols.	The child is told a letter name, and is shown the letter form. He is trained until he automatically selects the correct letter form when he hears its name.
12. *Motor response to an auditory stimulus.* The child responds motorically to a verbal command.	The child is told a letter name, and learns to immediately write that letter form.

Training Kinesthetic-Tactile Perception

The importance of kinesthetic-tactile perception has been stressed by Orton (111), Fernald (36), and Austin and Sleight (4). In our training program, we follow the guide lines below in developing kinesthetic-tactile perception.

1. Simple lines rather than widened ones are used. Very wide lines seem to confuse children.
2. Textured figures are better than nontextured. Texturing can be done by drawing the figure with liquid cement and covering it with fine sand.
3. We do not approve of the extensive use of highly raised or grooved figures.
4. Most of the figures used should be of alphabetic or digital types.
5. The tracing material should be so mounted that the child cannot change the material's position after his best perceptual angle has been determined by the educational therapist.

Training Auditory Perception

In our work with children who have difficulty with auditory discrimination, we follow these guide lines:

1. If the child is severely handicapped in this area, instruction is needed at the gross auditory-discrimination level. The

child is given experiences with sounds such as clapping, tapping, finger snapping, whistling, running water, scrapping, musical notes, sounds of different musical instruments, etc. We have found that it is a good idea to tape record a series of sounds for use at this level.

2. The next training stage involves the use of meaningful words. The child should learn to tell whether two words are alike or different, if two words rhyme or not, and to supply a rhyming word for one given to him.

3. Next, the child should learn to differentiate between, and reproduce, letter names.

4. At this point, the child should be ready to discriminate between, and reproduce, consonant sounds.

5. Finally, the child should be taught to discriminate between, and reproduce, long vowels, short vowels, and the *schwa* sound.

6. Auxillary hearing aids, such as watching the teacher's lips, feeling of the teacher's lips and throat, and the child's watching his own speech performance in a mirror, should be used in the early part of the training.

Training Visual Perception

The importance of visual perception has been noted by Bowden (18), Gates and Boeker (50), Gates (42), Davidson (28), Gellerman (52), Wilson and Fleming (152), Fernald (36), Newson (109), Piaget and Inhelder (114), Cruickshank, Bice and Wallen (26), and Ashlock (3).

In our work with children who have visual perceptual problems, we follow these guide lines:

1. We deal with three types of visual perceptual material. We teach them in the following order:
   a. Meaningful pictorial material.
   b. Digital and geometric material.
   c. Alphabetic material.

2. To aid the child in the initial stages of visual perceptual training, we make use of white figures on a black background. For example, we work with white chalk on an old-fashioned blackboard, use white India ink on black construc-

tion paper, and have materials commercially printed by the reverse printing process which results in white print on black paper.

The sensory and perceptual build-up is one of the most important parts of educational therapy for many children. The therapist should make sure that the child does not begin remedial instruction until sensory and perceptual skills are as near up to par as possible.

Chapter VI

THE LEARNING BUILD-UP

MOST CHILDREN who have learning problems are characterized by the presence of one or both of the following dilemmas:

1. They have never established a style or pattern of learning.
2. The patterns which they have established are so inadequate and/or inflexible that they cannot stand up under the increasing demands of school work.

Have you ever watched one of these youngsters try to "study?" He opens his book (probably to the wrong page). He checks with his neighbor to see if he is in the right place. He "reads" for a while. He gets up to sharpen his pencil. He looks at his book again. He looks out of the window. Eventually, he finishes "reading" the assignment. And that is it. No real study. No review. No comparison of new ideas with old. No attempt to logically organize the new concepts involved.

Before going into the ways educational therapists can help a child develop a style or pattern of learning, let us review a few basic principles of learning:

1. What is expected of a child must be justified in terms of what is known about his learning ability. It is harmful to set goals which the child cannot attain. It is equally harmful to set goals which are too low to give the bright child real challenge and satisfaction.
2. When a child is motivated, he learns more easily than when he is not motivated.

3. Motivation arising from within the child is better than that supplied by the adult.

4. Reward is usually better than punishment, but punishment is better than having a learning situation with no controls at all.

5. The child needs to be told about the quality of his performance.

6. Children must develop realistic concepts of themselves as learners—neither expecting too little nor too much of themselves.

7. Children can usually face failure better if they have had some successes in the past to build them up.

8. Some children learn more effectively with one teacher than another, and some teachers work better with some children than with others.

9. Active learning is better than passive learning.

10. It is easier to learn meaningful material than unfamiliar material.

11. It is easier to learn concrete material than abstract material.

12. Some learning tasks, such as arithmetic facts and spelling words, must be "overlearned." For this, drill is necessary.

13. Children need to discover relationships for themselves, and to apply old learnings to new situations.

14. Children need to feel the security of a structured, controlled learning situation.

15. Children, especially children with learning problems, need to feel that the teacher knows what he is doing.

Identifying the Preferred Sensory Modalities for Learning Reading and Spelling

We believe that the educational therapist should try to determine by which combination of sensory modalities (sight, hearing, touch, and muscular movement) the child seems to learn most easily. Ashlock (2) has theorized that children may vary significantly in the combination of sensory modalities through which it is easiest for them to learn symbolic material. While experience in school seems to cloud over the child's original preferred learning plan, it is the educational therapist's responsibility to try to rediscover it.

In Ashlock's summarization of the historical antecedants of his thesis, he concluded that teaching material of a symbolic nature has historically been accomplished through the following sensory approaches:

1. Visual-auditory.
2. Visual-auditory-kinesthetic.
3. Auditory-kinesthetic.
4. Tactile-kinesthetic.
5. Visual-auditory-kinesthetic-tactile.

In his summarization of his review of the literature on this subject, Ashlock said the following:

> There is a long history of educational techniques which are directly or indirectly based upon the thesis that children differ in preferred sensory modalities for learning symbolic material. Some empirical data seems to confirm this thesis.
>
> There is a paucity of experimental research dealing directly with the thesis or with the educational techniques based upon it. While the field of special education has concerned itself with the thesis, little has been done in the area of preferred sensory modalities when gross sensory defects have not been present.
>
> There is some evidence which indicates that a particular sensory modality does not develop at an equal rate in all children, and that the various sensory modalities do not develop at the same rate in a particular child.

We believe that much is to be gained at this point by the educational therapist's making a preliminary determination of preferred sensory modalities. This is where *diagnostic teaching* comes in. The educational therapist teaches a series of trial lessons which bring into use different combinations of sensory modalities. Notes on the effectiveness of the different methods are kept. In this way the educational therapist has some basis for deciding which approach is best for this particular child.

For example, the therapist might determine in the following manner which is the best way to teach a child reading:

1. The therapist selects reading material which is at the child's instructional level. The material is divided so that it is in three sections of approximately equal length. In each divi-

sion there should be enough material for at least three separate sessions.

2. The therapist begins with about three lessons using the visual-auditory approach. This is the traditional "look-say" method. If the child does not know a word, the teacher pronounces it for him, and he repeats it. Or, a combination of the look-say and the phonics approach can be used. If the child does not have a hearing deficit or a severe auditory perceptual problem, we always recommend a combination of the look-say and the phonic method.

3. Next, the therapist tries about three lessons using the visual-auditory-kinesthetic method. In this approach, the visual-auditory method is reinforced by such kinesthetic activities as using a pencil to trace or copy the words and/or phonic elements which are giving the child trouble.

4. Last, the therapist tries about three lessons using the visual-auditory-tactile-kinesthetic approach. In using this method, the sense of touch is used to reinforce the learning which is taking place. The child traces words and/or phonic elements with his finger tip as well as with a pencil. The most highly structured method of this type is that developed by Fernald (36).

The therapist should keep notes on his objective and subjective impressions of the child's performance when taught by each of the three methods. The child's preference should also be noted. Then the educational therapist should select the method that he will recommend to the teacher, or which he himself will use if he assumes the role of remedial teacher.

Due to the nature of the skills involved, the process of selecting a preferred sensory modality is of use primarily in the areas of reading and spelling. It should be noted, however, that in the teaching of handwriting, it is often necessary for a child to use finger and pencil tracing of letter forms in order to learn how to form the characters correctly.

Selecting the Best Approach to Handwriting

1. *Handedness.* The approach to be used depends on whether the child is right or left handed. For children who are left

handed, we recommend the *Left Handed Writing Instruction Manual* by Gardner (41).

For the child who is right handed, almost any standard approach is acceptable.

2. *Degree of Visual Acuity and Perception.* For the child who has difficulties of a visual acuity or perceptual nature, we recommend Sight Saving Paper from Stanwix House or Imaginary Line Handwriting Paper from the Steck-Vaughn Company.

Selecting the Best Approach to Teaching Arithmetic

While the success of reading and spelling instruction is highly dependent upon the correct utilization of the preferred sensory modalities, the approach to arithmetic has its foundations in the area of conceptualization. This helps explain why there is often little correlation between a child's achievement in reading and in arithmetic.

In deciding upon the best approach to teaching the child arithmetic, we have to decide his preference for alternative arithmetical processes and the degree of concreteness needed to teach him.

As has been indicated in the principles of modern math, a child should be taught that there may be two or three ways of carrying out an operation, but that he should be able to choose the way which is best for him. In doing diagnostic teaching of arithmetic, the teacher should also make note of just how concrete the teaching aids must be in order for the child to learn effectively.

Describing the Child's Best Approach to the Content Areas

The content areas, such as social studies and science, have in common the necessity for continually learning new concepts. It is important for the educational therapist to describe the most effective way for the child to approach conceptual learning in each particular field of context study. Some of the aspects of a child's approach to conceptualization are:

1. *Preference for inductive or deductive thinking.* Does the child learn concepts best when he starts with a fact and works

toward a generalization, or when he starts from the generalization and reasons toward the particular?

2. *Level of creativity in dealing with concepts.* Is the child very creative in adding to and evaluating the teacher's presentation, or does he need extra help in seeing relationships and implications?

3. *Motivational level.* It is important that the educational therapist describe the child's level of interest in the subject matter to be learned.

Describing the Child's General Style of Learning

The educational therapist should summarize in a narrative fashion the child's style of learning. This description should include, where applicable, a discussion of the preferred sensory modalities for learning reading and spelling, a selection of the best approach to handwriting, facts pertinent to the teaching of arithmetic, and a description of the best approach to the different content areas.

The Value of Diagnostic Teaching in the Learning Build-Up

The child's experiences in the diagnostic teaching which precedes the description of the style of learning are of central importance in the learning build-up. In providing the child with diagnostic learning experiences, we are asking him to work at his own level of ability; we are trying to motivate the youngster; we are giving him feedback concerning the quality of his performance; we are helping him develop a realistic concept of himself as a learner.

Chapter VII

THE EMOTIONAL AND BEHAVIORAL
BUILD-UP

WHEN A CHILD is brought to us for educational therapy, we find that we usually have an emotionally hurt child on our hands. He may be quiet and withdrawn, afraid to do anything which will make him feel more inadequate than he does already. He may be belligerent and exhibit a "try and teach me" attitude. He may simply "not give a damn." He may deny that he has a learning problem. The following conversation between one of the authors and a child who was doing very poorly in school, in his family relationships, and in his relationships with his peers is illustrative of how confused these children can become:

Therapist: "How are you doing in school?"

  Joe: "Fine."

Therapist: "What about reading?"

  Joe: "Fine."

Therapist: "Is there anything in school that is giving you trouble?"

  Joe: "No."

Therapist: "Then why are you here?"

  Joe: "My mother brought me."

Therapist: "Why did your mother bring you to see me?"

  Joe: "Because I don't read so good."

Therapist: "But you just told me that you read fine."

  Joe: "Well, my mother doesn't think so."

Therapist: "Well, just exactly what do you think?"

  Joe: "I don't know—I'm sort of mixed up."

As the first step in the emotional build-up of a child in educational therapy, the therapist should ask himself, "What are this child's emotional needs in connection with his learning problem?" Some common emotional and behavioral needs of children who have learning problems are:

1. Adult control.
2. Acceptance by parents and teachers.
3. Adult approval.
4. Identification with one's culture, past and present.
5. Experiences with both reward and punishment.
6. A feeling of protection, not overprotection, by adults.
7. Submission to authority.
8. Understanding of one's environment.
9. Peer approval.
10. Companionship.
11. Establishment of relationships with significant members of both sexes.
12. Consistency in interpersonal relations.
13. Honesty in relations with other people.
14. Taking care of other people.
15. Affiliation of oneself with other individuals and with groups of individuals.
16. Self control.
17. Self confidence.
18. Self acceptance.
19. Sense of accomplishment.
20. Internal drive.
21. Ways of dealing with guilt feelings.
22. Sense of duty.
23. Challenge.
24. Appropriate level of anxiety.
25. Reduction of frustration.
26. A degree of stress which can be handled.
27. Self expression.
28. Affection.
29. Agression.
30. Self actualization.
31. Defense of oneself.

32. Avoidance of harm.
33. Dominance of one's environment.
34. Order in one's environment.
35. Recreation.
36. Achievement.
37. Ability to concentrate.
38. Appropriate level of aspiration.
39. Realistic self concept as a learner.
40. Modification of the environment so that one can experience new learning which can replace inappropriate learnings which have already taken place.

In preparing the child for remedial instruction, we must begin to fulfill at least some of his emotional needs. Learning experiences have to be planned for the child so that he can get some emotional satisfaction from them. In planning such activities, we suggest that these general principles be followed:

1. Make the task easy enough to be accomplished, but difficult enough to be challenging.
2. The adult should give genuine approval if the child's performance merits it.
3. The child should be recommended for peer approval if
   (a) he deserves it, and
   (b) there is a good chance that the group will give it.
4. Call to the child's attention that he is doing a good or poor job.
5. Establish clear-cut standards of behavior and academic achievement. Enforce them. Give the child the security of knowing exactly where he stands, and that the emotional climate is reasonably steady and consistent.
6. Try to help the child internalize these standards or reasonable ones of his own making.
7. Make it clear that you accept the child, even though you may not accept all of his behavior. If you really do not like the child, or if he really cannot stand you, get him transferred to another educational therapist.
8. In discussing with a child his emotions, be specific, not general.
9. In the diagnostic teaching situation, the educational ther-

apist's methods should be consistent and structured, but not rigid.

10. Explain to the child the reasons for behavioral standards.
11. Isolate hyperactive children so that group disturbance will be at a minimum.
12. Allow a reasonable amount of physical movement.
13. Try not to be a perfectionist.
14. Stress the idea that the class is a team.
15. Stress the idea that each member of the class is responsible for his part in group activities.
16. As far as possible, teach academic material with the child's own needs in mind.
17. A sense of humor on the part of the educational therapist can reduce the child's anxiety.
18. Use clear directions.
19. In motivating the excitable child, do not overstimulate him.
20. Always keep in mind that children in need of an emotional and behavioral build-up have the same needs as average children; the needs of our children are just more intense.

The Flexibility of Emotional and Behavioral Management

In building up the child emotionally and behaviorally, the educational therapist should select a large number of diagnostic learning tasks for the child. In teaching, the therapist should try to follow the relevant principles listed previously in fulfilling the needs of the child. We must keep in mind that the needs of the child differ from time to time and from situation to situation. Flexibility based upon consistency of educational and psychological principles is important. In teaching a child to discipline himself, it is not important that the educational therapist win every battle—only that he win the war.

Chapter VIII

THE TRANSFER INTO REMEDIAL INSTRUCTION IN THE SKILL SUBJECTS

IT IS NOT the responsibility of the educational therapist to undertake remedial instruction unless the therapist is playing the dual role of educational therapist and remedial teacher. Usually, the educational therapist describes the problem, builds the child up for remedial instruction, and makes the transfer into remedial instruction. The child needs to get a taste of successful remedial experience before the educational-theraputic relationship is ended. These transfer lessons should be easy, but challenging. They should be geared to the interests of the child as far as this is reasonable.

Reading

After the reading level has been determined through the use of some of the reading achievement tests described in Chapter III, reading material should be selected which is in line with the child's interests. Of course, this can be overdone. Some children will never find "just exactly" what they are looking for because they simply do not wish to read. In such a case, the educational therapist will have to make the choice.

For this transfer work there are three primary objectives:

1. To develop some interest in the skill subject.
2. To build up a little confidence.
3. To make use of the proposed style or pattern of learning.

If commercial reading material is used, see that the child is only allowed to choose from material which is at least one year below the tested level of reading performance. Some suggested commercial materials for the teaching of reading are listed in Appendix A. Addresses of companies which publish materials referred to in this book will be found in Appendix B.

If the child would like to make up his own stories, he may dictate them to the educational therapist who can have them typed and return them to be read by the child. Do not be afraid of the "big" words. If they are in the child's speaking vocabulary, he can learn to read them.

Fernald (36) has made many helpful suggestions concerning child-dictated stories in her book, *Remedial Techniques in the Basic School Subjects*. If the child has a great deal of difficulty, the educational therapist may wish to use some of Fernald's techniques for word recognition.

If the educational therapist wishes to prepare his own material, he may wish to make use of one or more of the graded word lists available. We suggest the following:

1. *Basic Sight Vocabulary* (32)
2. *A Core Vocabulary* (136)
3. *A Reading Vocabulary for the Primary Grades* (43)
4. *The Teacher's Word Book of 30,000 Words* (139)

Handwriting

If the child is having trouble only with handwriting, concentrate on the cursive style. If the child is having difficulty with both reading and handwriting, begin work with the printed alphabet. This may strengthen the visual perception necessary for reading.

Whether printed or cursive characters are used, the following procedure can be followed. It is not necessary to go through all the steps with all children.

1. The teacher should guide the child through the finger-tracing of the character. The child should use the forefinger of the dominant hand. The teacher should be careful that the child traces the character in the correct direction.
2. The teacher should guide the child's hand as he writes the character.
3. The child copies the character by himself.

4. The child writes the character from memory.

For many useful hints on handwriting instruction, we refer the reader to Gray's UNESCO monograph, *The Teaching of Reading and Writing* (61).

In choosing a style of handwriting to be used, always follow the one that has been adopted by the child's permanent school. Otherwise, the youngster will be led into needless confusion.

The commercial materials for the teaching of handwriting which have been found to be of use to us are listed in Table II.

TABLE II

COMMERCIAL MATERIALS FOR TEACHING HANDWRITING

Material	Particular Merit or Value
1. The Imaginary Line Handwriting Program (Steck-Vaughn)	1. This program extends through the elementary grades, and is of particular value to children with learning problems of a visual perceptual nature. The extra guiding lines help the child to spatially orient manuscript and cursive letters.
2. Print-Script Word Builder (Houston)	2. Children learning to transfer from manuscript to cursive writing can compare and match the two styles of each letter. The disadvantage is that the letters are too small.
3. Left-Handed Handwriting (Interstate)	3. This is a common sense approach to teaching the left-handed child to write.

Spelling

It is our opinion that most poor spellers can trace at least part of their difficulty to a lack of phonic skills. For this reason, we recommend phonic-oriented teaching materials whenever the child has the necessary auditory perceptual skills to benefit from such an approach.

In addition, we have found the following spelling rules developed by Powell (86, p. 184) to be useful:

1. Correct pronunciation of the word by teacher and pupil is of primary importance.
2. Correct visual perception is important; in fact, Gilbert (53) says that correct perceptual analysis is characteristic of good spellers and can be improved in poorer spellers.
3. Knowing the meaning of the word being spelled is an advantage.

4. Longer words should be carefully pronounced by syllables although some words may be better left without too much emphasis on syllables.
5. Emphasis should always be placed on writing the word rather than on reading the letter sequence.
6. The amount of repetition necessary to learn will vary for different children and for different words. Learning to the point of being able to write the word correctly is not enough. Adequate learning is shown by the ability to write the word correctly several times in succession and also after an interval of at least several hours.
7. Time need not be spent on words completely memorized. Occassional reviews are helpful, but more time should be spent on learning difficult and doubtful words.

The commercial materials listed in Table III are useful in the teaching of spelling.

TABLE III

COMMERCIAL MATERIALS FOR TEACHING SPELLING

Material	*Characteristics*
1. *Developing Spelling Power* (123)	1. This is both a phonic and a visual approach to spelling. It is highly structured and can be of great value to the educational therapist who is not sure of how to structure such a program.
2. *Basic Goals in Spelling* (82)	2. This series is useful because it can be used to develop word meanings as well as word spelling.
3. *Spelling for Word Mastery* (113)	3. This is an excellent series because of its layout, its emphasis upon word meaning, and its use of word analysis techniques.
4. *Word Watching* (39)	4. This spelling program is based upon the principle of tachistoscopic presentation. For the child with good visual perception, it is a highly motivating method.
5. *My Word Book* (120)	5. This series is especially valuable because of the use that is made of structural linguistic principles.

Mathematics

We believe that there are four main causes of difficulty with mathematics:

1. Inadequate learning of the basic arithmetic facts and operations.

2. Reading difficulty in connection with story problems and directions.
3. Inadequate perception of spatial relationships. Stern (132) has devoted much of her book, *Children Discover Arithmetic,* to the importance of spatial concepts in arithmetic.
4. Carelessness.

In view of the transition which is now taking place in this country from the traditional arithmetic to the New Math, we do not recommend that the educational therapist invest money in new commercial teaching aids which are based upon the old method. Instead, we recommend that the therapist make use of aids already on hand, or help the child make the transition into the New Math. At this time, it would seem that educational therapists should begin learning one or more of the New Math programs.

Chapter IX

THE TRANSITION INTO REMEDIAL INSTRUCTION IN THE SUBJECT AREAS

REMEDIAL INSTRUCTION in the subject areas differs from remedial instruction in the skill subjects in a number of ways:

1. The skill subjects form a foundation upon which knowledge of the subject areas is based.
2. The skill subjects deal to a great extent with *perceptual* skills, while the subject areas deal primarily with *conceptual* skills.
3. Difficulty in the subject areas is usually due to
   (a) a faulty base upon which to build new concepts.
   (b) difficulty in comprehending new concepts.

The primary responsibility for instruction in the subject matter areas lies with the subject matter teacher. The task of the educational therapist in this area is only to stimulate the child's interest and help him establish some working plan.

Children who have adequate preparation in the necessary skill subjects, but who have difficulty in a subject matter area, can usually trace this condition to one or more of the following reasons:

1. Lack of interest in the subject matter.
2. Lack of identification with the methods of teaching.
3. Inadequate conceptual background.
4. Poor teaching which
   (a) does not take into account the interests of the child.
   (b) allows little or no pupil participation.
5. Inadequate classroom management.

When an educational therapist is preparing the child for work to be carried out by the subject matter teacher, the therapist should first try to discover any interests of the child which relate to the subject area. If interest can be found for any part of the subject matter, this interest should be stimulated and perhaps it will expand. Easy and interesting reading material should be provided along the lines of interest indicated by the child. Relevant field trips can be of great value.

Children who are having trouble with subject matter are often simply rebelling against the way it is being taught. For instance, children with a high need for physical movement will find it easier to learn by the project method than by the lecture method. The child who feels a preference to discuss and question concerning the subject matter will have difficulty if the class is too highly teacher-structured. Children who are by choice inductive thinkers will have difficulty when teaching is based entirely upon the deductive method and vice versa. Children who learn best through the visual channel will resent the straight lecture method. Children who learn best auditorily will be frustrated if the class presentation is heavily visual. The educational therapist should try to describe how the child learns best and relate this to the subject matter teacher.

Children come to a subject matter class with various conceptual backgrounds. When the child does not have the conceptual background for the subject matter taught, there are two things that can be done. Either special help must be given to develop in the child the conceptual background he needs, or the curriculum for the child can be so altered as to match his level of conceptual development.

We must face the fact that some children do not operate well in the subject areas because of poor teaching. The teacher who has no idea of the child's interests, the teacher who does nothing to enliven a dead textbook, the teacher who makes no effort to correlate the curriculum and the child's level of development, the teacher who is insecure, and the teacher who cannot maintain classroom discipline is not in a position to help the child who is having difficulty in the subject matter areas.

It must be noted, however, that there are limits as to how far the teacher can go in adjusting the subject matter curriculum to the interests and needs of each child. A class program must be maintained, and it is never possible for a teacher to be so flexible that he can meet all the needs of every child. Also, a class in which self-expression and child activity have gone so far as to turn the room into a playground is simply the reflection of the work of a weak teacher. Each teacher has to determine for himself just how far he can reasonably go in individualizing the curriculum according to the needs, interests, and conceptual background of each student.

Chapter X

EVALUATION

IN A FIELD as new as educational therapy, the problem of evaluation is very difficult. An educational field in its infancy must first define its goals and establish its definitions. Then it must proceed toward adapting old diagnostic instruments and inventing new ones. Treatment methods from other disciplines must be adapted, and new ones formulated. Only then can an infant field turn its attention to evaluation. At the present time, we offer the following suggestions for evaluating the progress of children who are in educational therapy. We hope that soon more helpful suggestions can be given.

Evaluation is actually the final step in the process of measuring the attainment of the goals of educational therapy. Evaluation is the process of interpreting both measurement of progress and subjective appraisals of progress.

Measurement

Measurement takes place when standardized tests are administered at the beginning and the end of the educational-theraputic process. The test scores are compared and the measurement of progress or regression is obtained by computing the difference between the two test scores. When possible, alternate forms of the same test should be given. If alternate forms are not available, the publishers should be consulted as to how much time should elapse between the first and second administration of the test.

Subjective Appraisal

Due to the newness of the field, we do not have as many standardized tests as we would wish to have. Consequently, the educational therapist must give his opinion as to how much progress the child has made in certain areas of educational therapy. When so doing, the therapist should give as many reasons as possible to support his subjective appraisal; for instance, he could say, "Johnny's motor coordination appears to have improved as a result of educational therapy because when he came to us he could not . . . and now he can. . . ."

Evaluation

This may well be the highest example of the therapist's art and skill. The educational therapist must bring together the results of measurement and subjective appraisal and interpret them in the light of all he knows about the educational problem of the child. In stating his evaluation, the educational therapist must assume full responsibility for his statements and subordinate his conclusions to those of no other discipline.

REFERENCES

1. Anderhalter, O., and Colestack, Ruth: *Scholastic Reading Readiness Test.* Chicago, Scholastic Testing Service, 1960.
2. Ashlock, P.: *Preferred Sensory Modalities for Learning Symbolic Material.* Unpublished manuscript.
3. Ashlock, P.: *Visual Perception of Children in the Primary Grades and its Relation to Reading Performance.* Austin, University of Texas Library; Ann Arbor, Michigan, University Microfilms, 1963.
4. Austin, T. R., and Sleight, R. B.: Accuracy of tactual discrimination of letters, numerals, and geometric forms. *J. Expt. Psychol., 43*:239–247, 1952.
5. Ayers, L. P.: *Measuring Scale for Handwriting: Gettysburg Edition.* Princeton, Educational Testing Service, 1912–40.
6. Baker, H. J. and Leland, Bernice: *Detroit Tests of Learning Aptitude.* Cincinnati, Public School Publishing Co., 1958.
7. Bateman, Barbara: *The Illinois Test of Psycholinguistic Abilities in Current Research: Summaries of Studies.* Urbana, University of Illinois Press, 1965.
8. Bender, Lauretta: *A Visual Motor Gestalt Test and its Clinical Use.* New York, American Orthopsychiatric Association, 1938.
9. Bender, Lauretta: *Bender Motor Gestalt Test: Cards and Manual of Instructions.* New York, The American Orthopsychiatric Association, 1946.
10. Benton, A. L.: Development of finger-localization capacity in school children. *Child Develop., 26*:225–230, 1955.
11. Benton, A. L.: *Right-left Discrimination and Finger Localization.* New York, Hoeber, 1959.
12. Benton, A. L., Hutcheon, J. F., and Seymor, Elsie: Arithmetic ability, finger localization capacity and right-left discrimination in normal and defective children. *Amer. J. Orthopsychiat., 21*:756–766, 1951.
13. Benton, A. L., and Schultz, L. M.: Observations on tactual form

71

perception (stereognosis) in preschool children. *J. Clin. Psychol.,* 5:359–364, 1949.

14. Betts, E. A.: Visual perception in reading. *Education, 73:*575–582, 1953.

15. Betts, E. A.: *Foundations of Reading Instruction.* New York, American Book, 1957.

16. Bond, G. L.: The auditory and speech characteristics of poor readers. *Teach. Coll. Contr. Educ.,* No. 657, 1935.

17. Bond, G. L., and Tinker, M. A.: *Reading Difficulties: their Diagnosis and Correction.* New York, Appleton-Century-Crofts, 1957.

18. Bowden, J. H.: Learning to read. *Elem. Sch. J., 12:*21, 1911.

19. Bower, E.: *The Early Identification of Emotionally Handicapped Children in School.* Springfield, Charles C Thomas, 1960.

20. Brueckner, L. J.: *Diagnostic Tests and Self-Helps in Arithmetic.* Los Angeles, California Test Bureau, 1955.

21. Cassidy, Rosalind: *Counseling in the Physical Education Program.* New York, Appleton-Century-Crofts, 1959.

22. Cattell, R. B., and Cattell, A. K. S.: *Cattell Culture Fair Intelligence Test.* Indianapolis, Bobbs-Merrill, 1960.

23. Catterall, C. D., and Weise, P.: A perceptual approach to early reading difficulties. *Calif. J. Educ. Res., 10:*212–219, 225, 1959.

24. Cavaletti, Sophia, and Gobbi, Gianna: *Teaching Doctrine and Liturgy.* New York, Alba, 1964.

25. Courtis, S. A.: The rate of growth makes a difference. *Phi Delta Kappan, 30:*316–323, 1949.

26. Cruickshank., W. M., Bice, H. V., and Wallen, N. E.: *Perception and Cerebral Palsy.* Syracuse, Syracuse University Press, 1957.

27. Dauer, V. P.: *Fitness for Elementary School Children Through Physical Education.* Minneapolis, Burgess, 1962.

28. Davidson, H. P.: An experimental study of bright, average and dull children at the four-year mental level. *Genet. Psych. Monogr., 9:*121–287, 1931.

29. De Hirsch, Katrina: Tests designed to discover potential reading difficulties at the six-year-old level. *Amer. J. Orthopsychiat., 27:*566–576, 1957.

30. Delacato, C. H.: *The Treatment and Prevention of Reading Problems.* Springfield, Charles C Thomas, 1959.

31. Delacato, C. H.: *The Diagnosis and Treatment of Speech and Reading Problems.* Springfield, Charles C Thomas, 1963.

32. Dolch, E. W.: *A Manual for Remedial Reading.* Champaign, Garrard Press, 1945.

33. Dunn, L. M.: *Peabody Picture Vocabulary Test*. Minneapolis, American Guidance Service, 1959.

34. Eisenson, J.: *Examining for Aphasia*. New York, Psychological Corporation, 1954.

35. English, H. B., and English, Ava C.: *A Comprehensive Dictionary of Psychological and Psychoanalytical Terms*. New York, McKay, 1958.

36. Fernald, Grace M.: *Remedial Techniques in Basic School Subjects*. New York, McGraw-Hill, 1943.

37. Fisher, Dorothy C.: *Montessori for Parents*. Cambridge, Bentley, 1965.

38. Fisher, Dorothy C.: *The Montessori Manual for Teachers and Parents*. Cambridge, Bentley, 1964.

39. Frackenpohl, Helen: *Word Watching*. Huntington, New York, Educational Developmental Laboratories, 1965.

40. Frostig, Marianne, in collaboration with Lefever, W., and Whittlessey, J. R. B.: *Administration and Scoring Manual for the Marianne Frostig Developmental Test of Visual Perception*. Palo Alto, Consulting Psychologists Press, 1964.

41. Gardner, W. H: *Left Handed Writing Instruction Manual*. Danville, Interstate, 1958.

42. Gates, A. I.: A study of the role of visual perception, intelligence, and certain associative processes in reading and spelling. *J. Educ. Psychol., 17:433–445*, 1926.

43. Gates, A. I.: *A Reading Vocabulary for the Primary Grades*. New York, Bureau of Publications, Teachers College, Columbia University, 1935.

44. Gates, A. I.: *Gates Reading Readiness Tests*. New York, Bureau of Publications, Teachers College, Columbia University, 1939 (Rev. 1942).

45. Gates, A. I.: *The Improvement of Reading*. New York, Macmillan, 1947.

46. Gates, A. 1.: *Gates Advanced Primary Reading Test*. New York, Bureau of Publications, Teachers College, Columbia University, 1958.

47. Gates, A. I.: *Gates Basic Reading Tests*. New York, Bureau of Publications, Teachers College, Columbia University, 1958.

48. Gates, A. I.: *Gates Primary Reading Test*. New York, Bureau of Publications, Teachers College, Columbia University, 1958.

49. Gates, A. I: *Gates Reading Survey*. New York, Bureau of Publications, Teachers College, Columbia University, 1958 (Rev. 1960).

50. Gates, A. I., and Boeker, E.: A study of initial stages in reading by pre-school children. *Teach. Coll. Rec., 24*:469–477, 1923.
51. Gates, A. I., and McKillop, Anne S.: *Gates-McKillop Reading Diagnostic Tests*. New York, Bureau of Publications, Teachers College, Columbia University, 1963.
52. Gellerman, L. W.: Form discrimination in chimpanzees and two-year-old children. *J. Genet. Psychol., 42*:3–50, 1933.
53. Gilbert, L. C.: An experimental investigation in learning to spell words. *Psychol. Monographs, 43* (1) : 1–82, 1932.
54. Gillingham, Anna, and Stillman, Bessie: *Remedial Training for Children with Specific Disability in Reading, Spelling, and Penmanship*. Cambridge, Educators, 1960.
55. Gilmore, J. V.: *Gilmore Oral Reading Paragraphs*. Yonkers, Harcourt, Brace & World, 1952.
56. Goins, J. T.: Visual perceptual abilities and early reading progress. *Suppl. Educ. Monogr.*, No. 87, 1958.
57. Goodenough, Florence.: *Goodenough Intelligence Test (Draw-a-Man)*. New York, Harcourt, Brace & World, 1926.
58. Grapke, M. F.: *Institute of Child Study Security Test*. Toronto, Guidance Centre, Ontario College of Education, University of Toronto, 1957.
59. Gray, W. S.: *On Their Own in Reading*. Chicago, Scott, Foresman, 1948.
60. Gray, W. S.: *Gray Oral Reading Paragraphs*. Cincinnati, Public School Publishing Co., 1955.
61. Gray, W. S.: *The Teaching of Reading and Writing*. Chicago, Scott, Foresman, 1956.
62. Group B of the Suburban School Study Council, Educational Service Bureau, School of Education, University of Pennsylvania: *Pupil Adjustment Inventory*. Boston, Houghton Mifflin, 1957.
63. *Group Test of Reading Readiness: The Dominion Tests*. Toronto, Guidance Centre, Ontario College of Education, University of Toronto, 1954.
64. Harris, A. J.: *How To Increase Reading Ability*. New York, McKay, 1961.
65. Harris, A. J.: *Effective Teaching of Reading*. New York, McKay, 1962.
66. Harrison, M. Lucile, and Stroud, J. B.: *Harrison-Stroud Reading Readiness Tests*. Boston, Houghton Mifflin, 1949–56.
67. Helson, H. (Ed.) : *Theoretical Foundations of Psychology*. New York, Van Nostrand, 1951.

68. Hindman, D. A.: *Complete Book of Games and Stunts.* Englewood Cliffs, Prentice-Hall, 1956.

69. Jastak, J., and Bijou, S.: *Wide Range Achievement Test.* New York, Psychological Corporation, 1946.

70. Jay, Edity S.: *A Book About Me.* Chicago, Science Research Associates, 1952.

71. Jerome Study Group: *Montessori in the Home.* Bethesda, Elad, 1963.

72. Jolles, I.: A teaching sequence for the training of visual and motor perception. *Amer. J. Ment. Defic. 63:*252–255, 1958.

73. Kagerer, R. L.: The Relationship Between the Kraus-Weber Test for Minimum Muscular Fitness and School Achievement. Unpublished master's thesis, Purdue University, 1958.

74. Kelly, T. L., Madden, R., Gardner, E. F., and Terman, L. M.: *Stanford Achievement Test (1953 Revision).* New York, Harcourt, Brace & World, 1953.

75. Kent, Grace H.: *Series of Emergency Scales.* New York, Psychological Corporation, 1946.

76. Kephart, N. C.: *The Slow Learner in the Classroom.* Columbus, Merrill, 1960.

77. Kirk, S. A.: *Teaching Reading to Slow-learning Children.* Boston, Houghton Mifflin, 1940.

78. Kirk, S. A.: *Educating Exceptional Children.* Boston, Houghton Mifflin, 1962.

79. Kirk, S. A., and Johnson, G. O.: *Educating The Retarded Child.* Boston, Houghton Mifflin, 1951.

80. Kirk, S. A., and McCarthy, J. J.: The Illinois test of psycholinguistic abilities—an approach to differential diagnosis. *Amer. J. Ment. Defic., 66:*399–412, 1961.

81. Kottmeyer, W.: *Teacher's Guide for Remedial Reading.* St. Louis, McGraw-Hill, 1959.

82. Kottmeyer, W., and Ware, Kay: *Basic Goals in Spelling.* St. Louis, Webster, Division of McGraw-Hill, 1960.

83. Kraus, H., and Hirschland, R. P.: Minimum muscular fitness tests in school children. *Res. Quart., 25:*178–188, 1954.

84. Lee, J. M., and Clark, W. W.: *Lee-Clark Reading Readiness Tests.* Los Angeles, California Test Bureau, 1962.

85. Lindquist, E. F., and Hieronymus, A. N.: *Iowa Tests of Basic Skills.* Boston, Houghton Mifflin, 1955–56.

86. Louttit, C. M.: *Clinical Psychology of Exceptional Children.* New York, Harper, 1957.

87. Lowder, R. G.: *Perceptual Ability and School Achievement.* Available from Winter Haven Lion's Club, Winter Haven, Florida, 1956.

88. McCarthy, J. J., and Kirk, S. A.: *The Construction, Standardization and Statistical Characteristics of the Illinois Test of Psycholinguistic Abilities.* Urbana, University of Illinois Press, 1963.

89. McCarthy, J. J., and Kirk, S. A.: *Examiners Manual: Illinois Test of Psycholinguistic Abilities* (experimental edition). Urbana, University of Illinois Press, 1961.

90. McCarthy, J. J., and Olson, J. L.: *Validity Studies on the Illinois Test of Psycholinguistic Abilities.* Urbana, University of Illinois Press, 1964.

91. *Manual of Directions for Use with the Keystone Visual Survey Service.* Meadville, Keystone View, 1961 (Rev. 1964).

92. Monroe, Marion: *Children Who Cannot Read.* Chicago, University of Chicago Press, 1932.

93. Montessori, Maria: *The Absorbent Mind.* Madras, India, Theosophical, 1963.

94. Montessori, Maria: *The Child.* Madras, India, Theosophical, 1961.

95. Montessori, Maria: *The Discovery of Childhood.* Madras, India, Kalakshetra, 1948.

96. Montessori, Maria: *Dr. Montessori's Own Handbook.* New York, Schocken, 1965.

97. Montessori, Maria: *Education for a New World.* Madras, India, Kalakshetra, 1959.

98. Montessori, Maria: *The Formation of Man.* Madras, India, Theosophical, 1962.

99. Montessori, Maria: *The Montessori Elementary Manual.* Cambridge, Bentley, 1965.

100. Montessori, Maria: *The Montessori Method.* New York, Schocken, 1964.

101. Montessori, Maria: *Peace and Education.* Madras, India, Theosophical, 1965.

102. Montessori, Maria: *Reconstruction in Education.* Madras, India, Theosophical, 1961.

103. Montessori, Maria: *The Secret of Childhood.* Bombay, India, Orient Longmans, 1965.

104. Montessori, Maria: *Spontaneous Activity in Education.* New York, Schocken, 1965.

105. Montessori, Maria: *To Educate the Human Potential.* Madras, India, Kalakshetra, 1961.

106. Montessori, Maria: *What You Should Know About Your Child.* Madras, India, Kalakshetra, 1961.

107. Murphy, Helen A., and Durrell, D. D.: *Murphy-Durrell Diagnostic Reading Readiness Test.* New York, Harcourt, Brace & World, 1949.

108. *The New York State Physical Fitness Screening Test.* Albany, University of the State of New York, State Education Department, Division of Health, Physical Education, and Recreation, 1964.

109. Newson, E.: *The Development of Line Figure Discrimination in Pre-school Children.* Unpublished doctoral thesis, University of Nottingham, 1955.

110. Olson, W. C.: *Child Development.* Boston, Heath, 1959.

111. Orton, S. T.: *Reading, Writing, and Speech Problems in Children; A Presentation of Certain Types of Disorders in the Development of the Language Faculty.* New York, Norton, 1936.

112. Otis, A. S.: *Otis Quick-scoring Mental Ability Tests.* New York, Harcourt, Brace & World, 1954.

113. Patton, D. H., and Johnson, Eleanor M.: *Spelling for Word Mastery.* Columbus, Merrill, 1959.

114. Piaget, J., and Inhelder, B.: *The Child's Conception of Space.* London, Routledge & Kegan Paul, 1956.

115. Prudden, Bonnie: *Is Your Child Really Fit?* New York, Harper, 1956.

116. Radler, D. H., and Kephart, N. C.: *Success Through Play.* New York, Harper, 1960.

117. Rambush, Nancy M.: *Learning How to Learn.* New York, Taplinger, 1962.

118. Remmers, H. H., and Bauernfeind, R.: *SRA Junior Inventory.* Chicago, Science Research Associates, 1957.

119. Robbins, S. D., and Robbins, Rosa S.: *Robbins Speech Sound Discrimination and Verbal Imagery Tests.* Magnolia, Expression, 1958.

120. Rogers, D. C., Ort, L. L., and Serra, Mary C.: *My Word Book.* Chicago, Lyons and Carnahan, 1962.

121. Rose, Florence C.: The occurrence of short auditory memory span among school children referred for diagnosis of reading difficulties. *J. Educ. Res., 51:*459–464, 1958.

122. Roswell, Florence G. and Chall, Jeanne S.: *Roswell-Chall Diagnostic Test of Word Analysis Skills.* New York, Essay, 1956–58.

123. Russell, Karlene V.: *Developing Spelling Power.* New York, Harcourt, Brace & World, 1957.

124. Schoolfield, Lucille D., and Timberlake, Josephine B.: *Phono-visual Diagnostic Spelling Test.* Washington, Phonovisual Products, 1949.

125. Sievers, Dorothy J., McCarthy, J. J., Olson, J. L., Batemen, Barbara D., and Kass, Corrine, E.: *Selected Studies on the Illinois Test of Psycholinguistic Abilities.* Urbana, University of Illinois Press, 1963.

126. *Signs of Eye Trouble in Children.* New York, National Society for the Prevention of Blindness, 1957.

127. Smith, Nila B.: Matching ability as a factor in first-grade reading. *J. Educ. Psychol., 29:*560–571, 1928.

128. Spache, G.: *Spelling Errors Test.* Gainesville, Reading Laboratory, University of Florida, 1955.

129. Sperry, Bessie, Ulrich, D. N., and Staver, Nancy: The relation of motility to boys' learning problems. *Amer. J. Orthopsychiat., 28:* 640–646, 1958.

130. Standing, E. M.: *Maria Montessori: Her Life and Work.* New York, Mentor-Omega Books by New American Library of World Literature, 1957.

131. Standing, E. M.: *The Montessori Method: A Revolution in Education.* Fresno, Academy Library Guild, 1962.

132. Stern, Catherine: *Children Discover Arithmetic: An Introduction to Structural Arithmetic.* New York, Harper, 1949.

133. Strauss, A. A., and Lehtinen, Laura E.: *Psycho-pathology and Education of the Brain-injured Child.* New York, Grune & Stratton, 1947.

134. Sullivan, Elizabeth T., Clark, W. W., and Tiegs, E. W.: *California Test of Mental Maturity.* Los Angeles, California Test Bureau, 1957.

135. Sullivan, Elizabeth T., Clark, W. W., and Tiegs, E. W.: *California Short-form Test of Mental Maturity.* Los Angeles, California Test Bureau, 1963.

136. Taylor, S. E., and Frackenpohl, Helen: *A Core Vocabulary.* Huntington, Educational Developmental Laboratories, 1960.

137. Terman, E. L., McCall, W. A., and Lorge, I.: *Non-language Multi-mental Test.* New York, Bureau of Publications, Teachers College, Columbia University, 1958.

138. Terman, L. M., and Merrill, Maud A.: *Stanford-Binet Intelligence Scale.* Boston, Houghton Mifflin, 1961.

139. Thorndike, E. L., and Lorge, I.: *The Teacher's Word Book of 30,000 Words.* New York, Bureau of Publications, Teachers College, Columbia University, 1944.

140. Thorpe, L. P., Clark, W. W., and Tiegs, E. W.: *California Test of Personality.* Los Angeles, California Test Bureau, 1953.

141. Thorpe, L. P., Leferer, W., and Naslund, R. A.: *SRA Achievement Series.* Chicago, Science Research Associates, 1955.

142. Thorpe, L. P., Meyers, C. E., and Bonsall, Marcella: *What I Like To Do.* Chicago, Science Research Associates, 1954.

143. Thurstone, L. L., and Thurstone, Thelma G.: *SRA Tests of Educational Ability.* Chicago, Science Research Associates, 1958.

144. Thurstone, Thelma G., and Thurstone, L. L.: *SRA Primary Mental Abilities.* Chicago, Science Research Associates, 1946–58.

145. Vernon, M. D.: *Backwardness in Reading.* New York, Cambridge University Press, 1957.

146. Vernon, M. D.: The perceptual process in reading. *Read. Teach., 13*:2–8, 1959.

147. Votaw, D. F., and Moses, Peggy L.: *Reading Readiness Test.* Austin, Texas, Steck-Vaughn, 1957.

148. *Webster Speech Correction Guide.* St. Louis, Webster Division, McGraw-Hill, 1955.

149. Wechsler, D.: *Wechsler Intelligence Scale for Children.* New York, Psychological Corporation, 1949.

150. Wepman, J. M.: *Auditory Discrimination Test.* Chicago, Language Research Associates, 1958.

151. White, Verna: *Studying the Individual Pupil.* New York, Harper, 1959.

152. Wilson, F. T., and Flemming, C. W.: Letter consciousness of beginners in reading. *J. Genet. Psychol., 53*:273–285, 1938.

153. Young, R. V., Pratt, W. E., and Whitmer, C. A.: *American School Reading Readiness Tests.* Cincinnati, Public School Publishing Co., 1941–55.

154. Zedler, Empress Y.: *Listening for Speech Sounds.* New York, Harper, 1955.

APPENDIX A

RECOMMENDED COMMERCIAL MATERIALS AVAILABLE FOR SPECIALIZED READING INSTRUCTION

Skill Categories	Appropriate Instructional Materials by Levels		
	Build-up	Primary (Grades K-3) and Intermediate (Grades 4-5-6)	Professional Reading for the Teacher
Auditory Perception	Rhythm Band instruments (Creative Playthings, Beckley-Cardy, School Playthings)	Objects that Rhyme, Rhyming Pictures, Rhyming Puzzles—Primary (Ideal)	Kirk (72) pp. 55, 71, 152.
	Sounds Around Us & Poetry Time—record albums (Scott, Foresman)	Rhyming—workbook activities—Primary (Continental Press)	Kephart (76) p. 235.
	A Reading Readiness Program for the Mentally Retarded, Primary Level (Parkinson)	Beginning Sounds—workbook activities—Levels 1 & 2—Primary (Continental Press)	Gray (59) pp. 25, 138-142.
	Sound Cylinders (Creative Playthings)	Twenty Pictorial Rhyming Sound Cards, Thirty-three Pictorial Initial Consonant Cards, Let's Listen Cards—Kindergarten and First Grade (Steck)	Fernald (36) p. 176.
		What's Its Name?—Kindergarten Through Intermediate (University of Illinois Press)	Betts (15) pp. 129, 331-332, 347-353, 581, 639-641.
		Come and Hear—Primary (Follett)	Harris (64) pp. 230, 329, 363.
		Listening Aids Through the Grades—Primary and Intermediate (Bureau of Publications)	
Eye-Hand Coordination	Visual Motor Skills—workbook activities—Levels 1 & 2 (Continental Press)	The Slingerland Kit—Kindergarten, Primary & Intermediate (Educators)	Kephart (76) pp. 25, 28, 47, 48, 116, 133, 138.

Area	Materials / Activities	Materials	References
Visual Perception	Puzzle Inlays, Judyettes, Storyettes, Parquetry Blocks (Judy)	Magic Designer Geometric Insets, Etch a Sketch, Dressing Frames, Hammer Nail Design Board Set, Manipulative Lock Board, Cloth Books, Pounding Bench, Work Bench Standard Hammer and Nail Set, Masonite Sewing Cards, Magic Basic Form Board, Parquetry Blocks—Kindergarten, Primary & Intermediate (Creative Play-things)	Radler (116) pp. 91–92.
	Lacing Boot, Make-It Set, Jumbo Beads and Laces, Playschool Puzzles (Stone)		
	Coordination Board (Sifo)		
	Beads for Stringing, Cubicle Counting, Peg-boards, (Houston) Coordination Board (Sifo)		
	Trace and Color (Platt & Munk)		
	Peg Boards and Pegs, Kindergarten Beads (Paine)		
	Climbing Equipment (Community)		
	Visual Discrimination—workbook activities—Levels 1 & 2 (Continental Press)	Letter Cards, Large Letter Cards Basic Letter Shapes (Ideal)	Kephart (76) pp. 80, 150.
		Kinesthetic Alphabet (Stone)	Radler (116) pp. 53–61.
		Reading Aids Through the Grades—Kindergarten, Primary & Intermediate. (Bureau of Publications)	Gray (59) pp. 96, 142–146, 161–162, 174–177, 182, 208–209.
	Independent Activities—workbook activities—Levels 1 & 2 (Continental Press)	Design Cubes, Magnastiks, Color Top, Kaleidoscope with Interchangeable Head & Discs, Graded Cylinder Sets with Knobs, Teleidescope, Asymmetric Space Construction Kit, College Projection Set, Color Cone, Rubber Peg Board & Pegs—Primary & Intermediate (Creative Play-things)	Kirk (77) pp. 40, 53, 68, 152, 71.
	Frostig Program for the Development of Visual Perception (Follett)		

Appropriate Instructional Materials by Levels

Skill Categories	Build-up	Primary (Grades K-3) and Intermediate (Grades 4-5-6)	Professional Reading for the Teacher
Basic Sight Vocabulary	Filmstrips for Readiness (Educational Development Laboratories)		Fernald (36) pp. 165, 176.
	A Reading Readiness Program or the Mentally Retarded, Primary Level (Parkinson)		Betts (15) pp. 331–347, 581, 611–614.
	Exercises to develop visual discrimination for letter and word forms from *Getting Ready*—Primary Level—(Houghton Mifflin)		
		Popper Words—Sets 1 & 2, Basic Sight Vocabulary Cards, Picture Word Cards, Sight Phrase Cards—Primary (Garrard)	Bond and Tinker (17) pp. 247, 263, 269–274.
		Flash Words—Sets 1 & 2, Picture Words for Beginners, Picture Word Builder, Words That Go Together—Primary (Milton Bradley)	Kirk (77) pp. 121, 116.
		Family Picture Cards, Basic Word Cards—Primary (Steck)	Fernald (36) pp. 35–51.
		A Reading Vocabulary for the Primary Grades (Bureau of Publications)	Gray (59) pp. 44–52.
		A Core Vocabulary Consisting of A Basic Vocabulary for Grades 1-8 & An Advanced Vocabulary for Grades 9-13. (Educational Developmental Laboratories)	Harris (64) pp. 316, 357.
		Pre-Primer Words and Primer Words by Gelles Widmer (Houston)	Betts (15) pp. 577, 581–582, 588, 590, 591, 595–614, 644.

Word Attack Skills		
	Beginning to Read Picture Dictionary—Primary (Follett)	Kottmeyer (81) pp. 113–114.
	Reading Essentials Teaching Aids—Primary (Steck)	Gray (59) entire book.
	Developing Spelling Power—Primary & Intermediate—(World)	Betts (15) Chapter 24.
	Beginning Sounds, Levels 1 & 2; We Learn to Read, 2nd semester; Phonics Fun; A Trip Through Wordland—Primary (Continental)	Harris (64) Chapters 12, 13, and 14.
	Consonant Pictures for Pegboard, Initial and Final Consonant Charts, Blends and Digraphs for Pegboard, Blends and Digraph Charts, Vowel Charts, Vowel Pictures for Peg Board, Phonic Drill Cards, Phonic Talking Letters, Phonic Word Builder—Primary (Ideal)	Bond and Tinker (17) Chapter 12.
	What the Letters Say, Consonant Lotto, Vowel Lotto, The Syllable Game—Primary & Intermediate (Garrard)	Gates (45) Chapters 7, 8, 9, 10, and 11.
	Phonetic Word Builder, Embecco Phonetic Drill Cards, Phonetic Word Wheel, Phonetic Quizmo (Milton Bradley)	Monroe (92) pp. 116–136.
	Eye and Ear Fun—Primary and Intermediate (Webster)	Gillingham and Stillman (54).
	Ways to Read Words & More Ways to Read Words—Primary and Intermediate (Bureau of Publications)	Zedler (154) entire book.
	Reading Laboratory I: Word Games—Primary (Science Research Associates)	Kottmeyer (81) pp. 115–158.
	Phonics We Use—Primary & Intermediate (Lyons Carnahan)	

Skill Categories	Build-up	Appropriate Instructional Materials by Levels	
		Primary (Grades K-3) and Intermediate (Grades 4-5-6)	Professional Reading for the Teacher
		New Practice Readers—Primary & Intermediate (Webster)	
		Reading for Understanding—Intermediate (Science Research Associates)	
		Reader's Digest Skill Builders (Reader's Digest)	
		Words in Color—Primary and Intermediate (Learning Materials)	
		Controlled Reader—Primary and Intermediate (Educational Developmental Laboratories)	
		Remedial Reading Drills—Primary (George Wahr)	
		Reading with Phonics and accompanying workbooks—Primary (Lippincott)	
		Phonetic Keys to Reading—with accompanying workbooks—Primary and Intermediate (Economy)	
		Conquests in Reading—Intermediate (Webster)	
		Picture Phonic Cards, Rainbow Word Builders, Word Family Fun; UNO, a Phonic Game—Kenworthy Teaching Aids—Primary and Intermediate (Houston)	
		Hayes Phonics Workbooks—Primary (Houston)	
		Basic Phonics Series—Primary and Intermediate (Houston)	
		The Phonovisual Method—Primary through 4th Grade (Phonovisual)	

Word Attack, Comprehension, Oral Reading, and Reading Rate Skills.	Remedial Training for Children with Specific Disability in Reading, Spelling, and Penmanship by Gillingham & Stillman—Primary and Elementary (Educators)	
	Phono Word Wheels, Phonic Word Builders, Phonic Talking Letters, Phonic Drill Cards, Word Prefixes, Word Suffixes—Intermediate (Houston)	
	Reading Skill Text—Primary & Intermediate (Bobbs Merrill)	Gates (45) Chapters 12, 13, 14, and 15.
	Reading Laboratories—Primary & Intermediate (Science Research Associates)	
	Deep-Sea Adventure Series, Jim Forest Readers and Practice Books, Morgan Bay Mysteries, Reading Motivated Series—Primary and Intermediate (Harr Wagner)	Bond and Tinker (17) Chapters 10, 11, 13, 14, 15, and 16.
	McCall-Crabbs Standard Test Lessons in Reading—Intermediate (Bureau of Publications)	
	Gates-Peardon Practice Exercises in Reading—Primary and Intermediate (Bureau of Publications)	Harris (64) Chapters 15, 16, 17, and 18.
	Three-In-One Workbook—Primary and Intermediate (Charles E. Merrill)	Betts (15) Chapters 20, 21, 22, and 23.
	Diagnostic Reading Workbook—Primary and Intermediate (Charles E. Merrill)	Harris (65) entire book.

Skill Categories	Appropriate Instructional Materials by Levels		
	Build-up	Primary (Grades K-3) and Intermediate (Grades 4-5-6)	Professional Reading for the Teacher
		Iroquois Phonics Series—Primary (Charles E. Merrill)	Kottmeyer (81) Chapters 13, 14, and 15.
		Filmstrips for Practice in Phonetic Skills—Primary and Intermediate (Scott, Foresman)	
		Reading Thinking Skills—Primary and Intermediate. (Continental Press)	
		New Practice Readers—Intermediate (Webster)	
		High Interest Low Vocabulary Series—Primary and Intermediate (Beckley-Cardy)	
		Comprehension Power Series—Primary and Intermediate (Educational Developmental Laboratories)	
		Independent Activities—Kindergarten and Grade I (Continental Press)	
		Thinking Skills—Kindergarten and Grade 1 (Continental Press)	
		Structural Reading Series—Kindergarten through Grade 2 (Singer)	
		Keyboard Town Store—Intermediate (Parkinson)	
		Learning to Think Series—Primary (Science Research Associates)	

APPENDIX B
List of Publishers' Addresses

Academy Guild Press, 2430 East McKinley, Fresno 3, California
Academy Library Guild, Box 549, Fresno, California
Alba House, A Division of St. Paul Publications, Staten Island, New York 10314
American Book Company, 55 Fifth Ave., New York 3, New York
American Guidance Service, Inc., 720 Washington Ave. S.E., Minneapolis 14, Minnesota
American Orthopsychiatric Association, Inc., 1790 Broadway, New York 19, New York
Appleton-Century-Crofts, Inc., 440 Park Ave. S., New York, New York 10016
Beckley-Cardy, 1900 North Narragansett Ave., Chicago, Illinois 60639
Bentley (Robert), Inc., 18 Pleasant St., Cambridge, Massachusetts 02139
Bobbs-Merrill Company, Inc., 1720 East 38th St., Indianapolis 6, Indiana
Bureau of Publications, Teachers College, Columbia University, 525 West 120th St., New York 27, New York
Burgess Publishing Company, 426 South Sixth St., Minneapolis, Minnesota 55415
California Test Bureau, 5916 Hollywood Blvd., Los Angeles 28, California
Cambridge University Press, 32 East 57th St., New York, New York 10022
Community Playthings, Rifton, New York 12471
Continental Press, Inc., Elizabethtown, Pennsylvania 17022
Creative Playthings, Princeton, New Jersey 08540
Economy Company, 5811 West Minnesota, Indianapolis 41, Indiana
Educational Developmental Laboratories, Huntington, New York

Educational Testing Service, Princeton, New Jersey

Educators Publishing Service, 301 Vassar Street, Cambridge 39, Massachusetts

Elad Enterpreses, Bethesda, Maryland

Essay Press, Box 5, Planetarium Station, New York 24, New York

Expression Company, Magnolia, Massachusetts

Follett Publishing Company, 1010 West Washington Blvd., Chicago 7, Illinois

Garrard Press, 510–522 North Hickory St., Champaign, Illinois

Grune & Stratton, Inc., 381 Fourth Ave., New York 16, New York

Guidance Centre, Ontario College of Education, University of Toronto, 371 Bloor St. West, Toronto 5, Ontario, Canada

Harcourt, Brace & World, Inc., 757 Third Ave., New York, New York   10017

Harper & Brothers, 49 East 33rd St., New York 16, New York

Harr Wagner Publishing Company, 609 Mission Street, San Francisco 5, California

Heath (D. C.) & Company, 285 Columbus Ave., Boston 16, Massachusetts

Hoeber (Paul B.) , Inc., 49 East 33rd St., New York 16, New York

Houghton Mifflin Company, 2 Park St., Boston 7, Massachusetts

Houston Teacher Supply Company, Inc., 2405 San Jacinto, Houston, Texas

Ideal (See: American Desk Manufacturing Company, Temple, Texas)

Interstate Printers & Publishers, Inc., Jackson at Van Buren, Danville, Illinois

Judy Company, 310 North Second Street, Minneapolis 1, Minnesota

Kalakshetra Publications, Adyar, Madras 20, India *

Keystone View Company, Meadville, Pennsylvania

Language Research Associates, Box 95, 950 East 59th St., Chicago 37, Illinois

Learning Materials Inc., 100 East Ohio Street, Chicago 11, Illinois

Lippincott (J. B.) Company, East Washington Square, Philadelphia, Pennsylvania   19105

Longmans Green & Company, Inc., 119 West 40th St., New York 18, New York

Lyons & Carnahan, 2500 Prarie Ave., Chicago 16, Illinois

---

* Distributed in the U. S. by The Theosophical Press, P. O. Box 270, Wheaton, Illinois   60188.

McGraw-Hill Book Company, Inc., 330 West 42nd St., New York 36, New York

McKay (David) Company, Inc., 119 West 40th St., New York 18, New York

Macmillan Company, 60 Fifth Ave., New York 11, New York

Merrill (Charles E.) Books, Inc., 1300 Alum Creek Drive, Columbus 16, Ohio

Milton Bradley Company, Springfield, Massachusetts

National Society for the Prevention of Blindness, Inc., 1790 Broadway, New York 19, New York

New American Library of World Literature, Inc., 501 Madison Ave., New York 22, New York

Norton (W. W.) & Company, Inc., 55 Fifth Ave., New York 3, New York

Orient Longmans, Ltd., 17 Chittaranjan Ave., Calcutta 13, India *

Paine Publishing Company, 34 North Jefferson Street, Dayton, Ohio 45401

Parkinson (R. W.) and Associates, 704 Mumford Drive, Urbana, Illinois

Phonovisual Products, Inc., P. O. Box 5625, Friendship Station, Washington 16, D. C.

Platt & Munk Company, Inc., 200 Fifth Avenue, New York, New York, 10010

Prentice-Hall, Inc., Englewood Cliffs, New Jersey

Psychological Corporation, 304 East 45th St., New York 17, New York

Public School Publishing Company, 345 Calhoun St., Cincinnati 19, Ohio

Reader's Digest Services, Inc., Pleasantville, New York

Reading Laboratory, Anderson Hall, University of Florida, Gainesville, Florida

Routledge & Kegan Paul Ltd., 68–74 Carter Lane, London E. C. 4, England

Schocken Books, Inc., 67 Park Ave., New York 16, New York

Scholastic Testing Service, Inc., 3774 West Devon Ave., Chicago 45, Illinois

School Playthings, Inc., 1801 South Michigan Avenue, Chicago, Illinois 60616

Science Research Associates, Inc., 259 East Erie St., Chicago 11, Illinois

* Distributed in the U. S. by The Theosophical Press, P. O. Box 270, Wheaton, Illinois 60188.

Scott, Foresman & Company, 433 East Erie, Chicago 11, Illinois

Sifo (See: American Desk Manufacturing Company, Temple, Texas)

Singer (L. W.) Company, Inc., Division of Random House, Inc., 249 West Erie Boulevard, Syracuse, New York   13201

Stanwix House, Inc., Pittsburgh 4, Pennsylvania

Steck-Vaughn Company, 205 West Ninth St., Austin, Texas

Stone (R. H.) Products, Box 414, Detroit, Michigan   48231

Syracuse University Press, Box 87, University Station, Syracuse, New York   13210

Taplinger Publishing Company, Inc., 119 West 57th St., New York, New York

Theosophical Publishing House, Adyar, Madras 20, India *

Thomas (Charles C) Publisher, 301–327 East Lawrence Ave., Springfield, Illinois

University Microfilms, Inc., 313 North First St., Ann Arbor, Michigan

University of Chicago Press, 11030 South Langly, Chicago 37, Illinois

University of Illinois Press, Urbana, Illinois

University of the State of New York, The State Education Department, Albany, New York   12224

University of Texas Library, University of Texas, Austin, Texas

Van Nostrand (D.) Company, Inc., 120 Alexander St., Princeton, New Jersey

Wahr (George) Publishing Company, 316 South State Street, Ann Arbor, Michigan

Webster Division, McGraw-Hill Book Company, 1154 Reco Ave., St. Louis, Missouri   63126

Winter Haven Lion's Club, Winter Haven, Florida

* Distributed in the U. S. by The Theosophical Press, P. O. Box 270, Wheaton, Illinois 60188.

INDEX OF NAMES

INDEX OF REFERENCES

INDEX OF SUBJECTS

Date Due

MAR 3 1 '81			

BRODART, INC.   Cat. No. 23 233   Printed in U.S.A.